PAULINE JARICOT

BOOKS BY MARY FABYAN WINDEATT

In This Series

Stories of the Saints for Young People ages 10 to 100

THE CHILDREN OF FATIMA
And Our Lady's Message to the World

THE CURÉ OF ARS
The Story of St. John Vianney,
Patron Saint of Parish Priests

THE LITTLE FLOWER
The Story of St. Therese of the Child Jesus

PATRON SAINT OF FIRST COMMUNICANTS
The Story of Blessed Imelda Lambertini

THE MIRACULOUS MEDAL
The Story of Our Lady's Appearances
to St. Catherine Labouré

ST. LOUIS DE MONTFORT
The Story of Our Lady's Slave,
St. Louis Mary Grignion De Montfort

SAINT THOMAS AQUINAS
The Story of "The Dumb Ox"

SAINT CATHERINE OF SIENA
The Story of the Girl Who Saw Saints in the Sky

SAINT HYACINTH OF POLAND
The Story of the Apostle of the North

SAINT MARTIN DE PORRES
The Story of the Little Doctor of Lima, Peru

SAINT ROSE OF LIMA
The Story of the First Canonized Saint of the Americas

PAULINE JARICOT
Foundress of the Living Rosary and
The Society for the Propagation of the Faith

PAULINE JARICOT

FOUNDRESS OF THE LIVING ROSARY AND THE SOCIETY FOR THE PROPAGATION OF THE FAITH

By

Mary Fabyan Windeatt

Illustrated by

Paul A. Grout

TAN BOOKS AND PUBLISHERS, INC.
Rockford, Illinois 61105

Nihil Obstat: Francis J. Reine, S.T.D.
                    Censor Librorum

Imprimatur: ✠ Paul C. Schulte, D.D.
                    Archbishop of Indianapolis
                    Feast of St. Philomena
                    August 11, 1952

ISBN: 0-89555-425-9

Library of Congress Catalog Card No.: 93-60214

Printed and bound in the United States of America.

TAN BOOKS AND PUBLISHERS, INC.
P.O.Box 424
Rockford, Illinois 61105

1993

For all who have
given to the Missions,
whether at home or in faraway lands—
especially to those who have
given their lives.

DECLARATION OF OBEDIENCE

CONTENTS

CHAPTER 1

A YOUNG GIRL'S HEART

Anthony Jaricot was experiencing his usual temptation to pride as he walked up the center aisle of his parish church one Sunday morning in January, 1814, to attend High Mass with his family. How good to feel the hundreds of admiring eyes turned upon him! To know that he was one of the wealthiest and most respected men in Lyons! That his children were handsome, clever, well-educated and devoted to one another, and that he had the best wife in the world!

Then resolutely he put such thoughts aside. His reputation, his prospering silk business, his wife and family, were undeserved gifts from God. But for the goodness of Divine Providence, he might still be only a struggling factory hand, condemned to the poverty that had been the lot of so many in France since the Revolution twenty-five years before.

"Lord, forgive me!" he reflected soberly. "Everything I have is Yours. *Everything!*"

However, no such scruples bothered fourteen-year-old Pauline Jaricot as she followed her father up the aisle to their accustomed place. In fact, after the briefest of prayers, she settled back to enjoy the considerable flutter which the family's entrance had caused. On all sides necks were still being craned, and the girl's dark eyes glowed with excitement. Sunday was such a wonderful day! As usual, Mama looked elegant, this time in the dark green coat from Paris, with the ermine collar and cuffs. On all sides young women were gazing admiringly at Paul and Phileas, those two unmarried brothers who some day would inherit their share of the Jaricot fortune. But there was no use in pretending that she, Pauline, was not attracting envious glances, too—in her new pink wool, with a dashing little hat to match, trimmed with white rosebuds and a touch of ostrich plumes.

"If only Lucian likes it!" she thought hopefully, scarcely aware of the fact when the priest and his ministers entered the sanctuary and the organ intoned the Introit for the third Sunday after Epiphany. "Pale pink's the very latest thing." Then, with a frown: "But I should have worn another hat. This one's too much like Claire's, and she, poor girl, has no style at all. . . ."

An hour or so later, however, the horrid little qualm had been forgotten. Lucian was standing beside her on the church steps, loud in his praises of the new pink wool. *And* the hat.

"You're the prettiest girl in Lyons, Pauline," he confessed. "Everyone knows that."

Pauline dimpled demurely as Anthony Jaricot clapped the young man on the shoulder. "So, you still like our little girl, son? Well, just remember what I told you."

Lucian nodded eagerly. "Oh, yes, sir! I'm to work hard to prove myself. Then maybe some day—"

"Then maybe some day we'll give you our Pauline. Isn't that right, Joan?"

Madame Jaricot hesitated. "Maybe," she said slowly. But as some of the light faded from the boy's eyes, she smiled and stretched out her hand. "Lucian, why not spend the day

"YOU'RE THE PRETTIEST GIRL IN LYONS!"

3

with us?" she suggested. "Sophie and Laurette are coming for dinner, and some friends of Paul and Phileas, too. If you're not busy. . . ."

At once the boy's face brightened. "I'd like that very much, Madame. If . . . if it's all right. . . ."

"Of course it's all right!" boomed Anthony Jaricot. "There's nothing I like better on a Sunday afternoon than a house full of young folks having a good time. Come along, son. Our carriage is over this way."

For the rest of the day, because of Lucian's presence, Pauline was in a state of great excitement—enjoying the games, the singing and dancing, which were always included in a Sunday party at the Jaricot house. What a lucky girl she was! Why, her oldest sister Sophie had been nearly seventeen before she had found a husband in Zachary Perrin! Poor Laurette had been sadly close to twenty before Victor Chartron had claimed her as a bride. But she, Marie Pauline—

"I'll be married this summer, right after my fifteenth birthday!" she told herself happily. "Oh, dear Lord, how can I thank You for sending Lucian my way?"

But as spring approached and the Jaricots left their comfortable house in Lyons for Tassin, the beautiful country estate which had been purchased some two years before, Pauline's heart was often heavy. Although everyone else in the family approved of her marriage to Lucian, her mother had suddenly announced that she must wait a year or so before taking such an important step.

Pauline felt outraged. "But Mama, I *love* Lucian!" she had burst out tearfully. "And he loves me! Why can't you understand?"

Madame Jaricot only smiled. "Darling, I do understand. But you're still very young. And I don't want you to make any mistake. After all, it wasn't so very long ago when you thought you might like to be a nun. Remember?"

Pauline tossed her head. "A nun! That was ages ago, Mama, when I was only twelve—a mere child. Now I'm grown-up. I know what I want. Really!"

But Madame Jaricot was firm. A year would soon pass, she said. Lucian would be as welcome as ever as a guest, but there must be no more talk about an immediate wedding.

Poor Pauline! She had always been accustomed to having her own way, and for days after her fifteenth birthday she sulked about the house. Papa understood, she told herself. And Paul and Sophie and Laurette and Phileas. They saw nothing wrong with Lucian. He was wealthy, handsome, ambitious, well-educated, and very much in love with her. There was absolutely no reason why the two of them couldn't be married right away. Of course, she admitted, Lucian was not so religious, but what of that? He was a good boy. Everyone said so. He was just like so many other young men—not particularly given to church-going or praying in public.

"But he'll be converted after we're married," she assured herself. "I'll pray for him so hard that he'll have to be!" And at this thought a smile brightened her face and she felt for the ring which her beloved had given her, wrapped in a handkerchief and carefully hidden against her heart.

Of course it was not really an engagement ring, for it had belonged to Lucian himself. And of course no one knew that she had it, or that she had given a lock of hair in exchange. But it was a satisfactory substitute until that glorious day when

Mama would finally consent to a formal engagement and she, Pauline, might openly wear the beautiful diamond which Lucian would select.

And so the days of waiting passed uneventfully. Then presently a wholly unlooked-for accident occurred to fill Pauline with anxiety. Lucian's ring, wrapped in its handkerchief, went to the laundry and was returned by a puzzled maid to Anthony Jaricot when the whole family was at dinner.

"I don't know whose it is, sir, or where it comes from," she declared. "But it's certainly a man's ring. . . ."

Anthony examined the discovery carefully, then turned to his family. "Does this belong to any of you?" he asked.

Paul and Phileas, after a quick glance, denied ownership, and Pauline, her heart beating wildly, dared not say a word.

"Well, then, I'll just keep it myself," said Anthony, smiling. "It's something like a ring I lost some time ago."

Poor Pauline! For days she plotted how to recover her treasure. Of course the simplest thing would be to explain matters to her father privately. He, so fond of Lucian, would think it all a big joke, and return the ring at once. But then he might tell Mama everything, too, and Pauline shrank at the thought of another scene.

"What a careless little fool I was!" she told herself. "Now I'll just have to wait until Lucian can give me my own ring."

But as the days passed and one important social event after another occupied Pauline's time, the loss of the ring assumed less tragic proportions. Since she was young, rich and pretty, there were more invitations to receptions and parties than she could accept. And what a lot of time it took to prepare for them! Every week or so there were sessions with the dress-

maker and milliner, for it would never do to be seen twice
in the same outfit. Then there were also frequent visits to the
jeweler, for Anthony Jaricot was generosity itself where his
youngest daughter was concerned. Bracelets, necklaces, earrings
and brooches to match Pauline's dozens of costumes? Why, of
course! The finest stones in the world were none too good
for his little girl.

"Happy, child?" he asked from time to time, when, radiant
and lovely, his youngest daughter presented herself for his
approval.

Pauline always nodded eagerly. "Oh, yes, Papa! It's just
wonderful to be alive!" Then, with a wry little face: "But it'd
be even more wonderful if—well, you know what."

"If Mama would say 'yes'?"

"That's right. Oh, what a long time a year can be! Sometimes I don't think I can wait another day!"

CHAPTER 2

A DRASTIC CHANGE

Anthony's kind heart was troubled more than once by the longing in his daughter's eyes. But love and respect for his wife were deep, and therefore he tried his best to understand her unwillingness to have Lucian as a son-in-law until Pauline was at least sixteen. Then one day, while he was busy at his silk factory in Lyons, a message arrived to the effect that Pauline had suffered a painful accident. While standing on a high stool trying to reach the top shelf of a cupboard, she had fallen heavily to the floor. No bones seemed to be broken, but it might be well if he came home.

Greatly alarmed, Anthony set out at once. "Dear God, don't let this be serious!" he prayed. "Why, if anything should ever happen to my little girl. . . ."

When he arrived, it seemed as though the heartfelt prayer had been answered. Pauline herself was making light of the mishap and insisting that she had suffered no more than a few bruises. But presently she began to complain of a severe pain in her back.

"I ache all over!" she told the family. "And my legs don't feel right . . . or my arms either. . . ."

Madame Jaricot comforted her tenderly. "Darling, you must go to bed at once," she declared. "I'll nurse you myself until you're all well again."

Poor Pauline! She had never been really sick in all her fifteen years, and pain was something new to her. To make matters worse, the autumn social season was about to open, with its exciting round of banquets and dances, and at least a dozen new dresses were ready to be tried on, with their matching wraps.

"Mama, I just haven't the time to lie in bed!" she exclaimed impatiently. "I've got to be up and around!"

But the next morning the pain was so intense that Pauline could scarcely stand. Her arms and legs were half-paralyzed, and there was a nervous twitching in her face. Even her speech was affected.

The doctor was puzzled. "I don't understand what's wrong with the girl," he admitted. Then, as the Jaricot family looked at one another in dismay: "Sometimes, though, a case like this responds remarkably well to bleeding. Maybe we ought to try that."

So Pauline was "bled," but with most unsatisfactory results. For in a few days she no longer had the strength to get out of bed. Worse still, there was a faintness at her heart and the nervous spasms in her face, legs and arms became even more pronounced.

Madame Jaricot was beside herself with anxiety. "Maybe a visit from Lucian would help," she suggested desperately. "Oh, Anthony, if he or anyone else can do something for that poor child. . . ."

But Pauline refused to have any visitors—especially Lucian. "I don't want him to see me like this!" she sobbed. "Oh, Mama, I'm nothing but a wretched cripple! He . . . he'd be sick at the sight of me!" And she became so overwrought that Madame Jaricot was thoroughly alarmed.

"There, there, dear! You don't have to see Lucian, or anyone else, unless you want to."

For a moment Pauline stared at her, her face twitching nervously. Then slowly she closed her eyes. "It's a promise, Mama?" she whispered.

Madame Jaricot stroked her hair reassuringly. "Of course it's a promise, dear. Now, go to sleep and don't worry any more about anything."

Anthony Jaricot was half out of his wits with anxiety. And when, after some weeks, his wife collapsed from the fatigue and strain of nursing Pauline and had to take to bed herself, it was almost more than he could bear. Then one day the doctor announced that there was really nothing he could do for Pauline. Probably she would be an invalid for the rest of her days. Even worse, it was likely that her mind would be permanently affected.

"I've been giving her tests off and on, sir," he told Anthony, "and there's no doubt about it. The girl's brain was injured in that fall. I don't see how she can ever be normal again."

The father was heartbroken. "Oh, no, doctor! Not that!" he pleaded.

But the doctor shook his head gravely. "I'm sorry, sir. That's the way it seems to be."

The dreadful expectation weighed heavily upon the whole family. Pauline—so young, so pretty, and with everything to live for—was losing her mind? Oh, surely not!

"Dear Lord, do with me anything You wish, but spare my

child that cross!" begged Madame Jaricot from her sickbed. "Take my life... *anything* ... only let Pauline recover...."

The weeks passed, and there was no improvement in either of the invalids. Then one day the doctor decided that a change of scene might do Pauline good. And so, with great care and tenderness, she was taken from her home in Lyons to the country estate at Tassin.

"And my wife, doctor?" Anthony had asked when the move was suggested. "What about her?"

The latter hesitated. "Madame Jaricot had better stay where she is," he said finally. "Two sick people in the same house—well, they're not good for each other."

Contrary to everyone's impressions, Pauline was fully aware of what was taking place. On her first night at Tassin, she woke suddenly with the conviction that something was seriously wrong with her mother.

"Dear God, if she's ill, make her get better," she whispered weakly. "And if necessary, let me die in her place...." Then she drifted back into a fitful sleep.

But although Pauline's condition did improve somewhat in the days which followed, it remained very serious. She still suffered the jerky movements in her arms and legs, and her speech was thick and slow. Hence, no one dared tell her when her mother took a sudden turn for the worse; or, finally, that she had died. Indeed, when thirty-two-year-old Paul Jaricot was married to Julie Germain in June, 1815, not a word of it was mentioned to the young invalid. Any shock or emotional excitement, the doctor had warned, might prove fatal.

However, sixteen-year-old Pauline sensed that something was wrong. Depressed and in constant pain, she spent long hours staring at the ceiling. Most of the time she was too tired to cry, but occasionally when she was alone the bitter tears came in floods.

"E-everyone thinks I'm out of my mind," she realized desperately. "They've told Lucian, and he . . . he's fallen in love with another girl! That's why he never comes. . . ."

Poor Pauline! In the early days of her illness she had grown so disturbed at the thought of a visit from Lucian that, to spare her pain, the family had decided never to mention his name in her presence. But she had forgotten all this now, and since she was too proud to inquire about her beloved, no one ever guessed how much she longed for him.

"The poor, poor child!" groaned Anthony disconsolately. "What's to become of her?"

Then one day the parish priest came to Tassin for a visit. "Pauline, wouldn't you like to receive Holy Communion?" he asked. "I could hear your confession now. Then to-morrow. . . ."

Pauline stared at her visitor, then slowly shook her head. "Oh, Father, I couldn't!" she murmured weakly. "I'd be too afraid. . . ."

"Afraid? But why, little one? Our Lord loves you very much. And it's been such a long time since He came into your heart. . . ."

For a moment Pauline was silent. How could she ever admit to this good priest that she all but hated God for having allowed the dreadful accident to happen? How, whenever she saw herself in a mirror, so pale and ugly and useless, she felt like screaming? How she spent entire days envying her friends their health and high spirits? Their parties and dances and other good times? As for Lucian, whom she had loved and trusted more than anyone else in the whole world—

"Come, child, tell me all about it," said the parish priest solicitously. "You'll feel so much better afterwards."

Suddenly Pauline was sobbing as though her heart would break. "Oh, you'd never understand, Father! Y-you couldn't possibly know how bad I've been...."

CHAPTER 3

WAITING AND WONDERING

But the parish priest did understand. As gently as he could, he explained that God is not only a God of justice but a God of mercy, too. A Father, in the truest sense of the term. There had been some good reason why He had permitted the dreadful accident to happen. For the time being He seemed to want this to remain a secret, but some day all would be clear.

"Child, it could be that there's a great work in store for you," he said encouragingly. "Something you'd never have been able to do if you hadn't known real suffering first. So, cheer up. Everything's going to be all right."

Pauline wiped her tearful eyes. "B-but I'm not interested in a great work, Father!" she choked. "I just want to be like other girls . . . able to get about like I used to. I . . . I don't want to be different! Not the least little bit!"

The priest smiled. "*You* don't want to be different? Ah, I think it's the Devil who doesn't want that." And so persuasive were his words that finally Pauline agreed to go to confession and receive Holy Communion.

To everyone's joy and relief, the young invalid showed a vast improvement after the reception of the Sacraments. She slept much better at night and was far less moody. In a week or so she was even able to walk about without assistance, and

14

"I JUST WANT TO BE LIKE OTHER GIRLS. . . ."

15

finally it was considered safe to tell her of her mother's death nearly eight months before.

"I knew it all along," was Pauline's only comment. Then, a little later: "Poor Mama! I think she must have offered her life for me."

The Jaricots—Paul, Sophie, Laurette and Phileas—were jubilant over their young sister's remarkable recovery, and especially at the calmness with which she had received the news of her mother's passing. How terrible if she had gone to pieces and suffered a relapse! As for Anthony, he was beside himself with gratitude.

"Pauline's going to be all right after all," he assured himself. "Oh, thank God!"

During the following days, Pauline recovered her strength and spirits rapidly. How good it was first to be free from pain, then to walk normally, to speak clearly, to have the full use of her hands again, so that she could fix her hair in one becoming fashion after another! Then came the great joy of being able to resume her normal life, to visit her friends in Lyons, to feel herself the center of attraction wherever she went. . . .

Watching their youngest return to her carefree way of life, the Jaricots experienced a keen satisfaction. "It won't be long before there's a wedding," they told one another confidently. "Why, Pauline's even more attractive now than before her illness!"

But as the weeks passed and Pauline made no mention of Lucian—indeed, avoided his company completely—doubts arose. No one referred to the matter openly, but there were many secret discussions as to what was wrong.

"I know. Pauline's thinking of Mama," Sophie decided finally. "She doesn't want to have anything to do with Lucian out of respect for her memory."

"That's right," agreed Phileas. "Later on she'll be friends with him, though, just like in the old days."

"And a good thing, too," observed Paul. "He'll make her a splendid husband."

"He certainly will," said Laurette.

The family was mistaken, however. Pauline did miss her mother terribly. Over and over again she regretted the many scenes of which Lucian had been the cause. Yet it was not on this account that she made no mention of him. During the long months of illness, her feelings toward Lucian had undergone a critical change. Now she no longer cared whether she saw him or not.

"I just don't love anyone," she told herself, not without relief.

But this detachment did not last. In the midst of the gayest party, sixteen-year-old Pauline often felt like bursting into tears. How terrible to be so alone! So different from her friends! To want to fall in love after all, and yet to realize that there was no one to whom she could give her heart! Even worse. The nagging fear that there never would be anyone . . . that God did have some other plan for her. . . .

"I just *can't* be a nun!" she told herself tearfully. "I like going places too much, and having pretty clothes! I *couldn't* spend all my life shut up in a convent. . . ."

Yet suppose this was "the great work" which God had in store for her, and to which the parish priest had referred when he had come to hear her confession? Suppose that she would never know peace until she said "yes"?

As the weeks passed, Pauline's uneasiness about the future could not be entirely concealed, and her family began to be less certain that all was well with her. Then one day a solution to the problem presented itself. Twenty-six-year-old Sophie Jaricot (who had been married to Zachary Perrin for nine years) informed her young sister that she had met a saint in the person of Father John Wurtz.

"Pauline, he's going to preach at the High Mass next Sunday!" she burst out excitedly. "You simply must come and hear him!" And she began to explain how she had just been to confession to Father Wurtz, how wonderfully kind he had been, and how well he had understood all her problems.

Pauline smiled indifferently, but she agreed to accompany Sophie to church the next Sunday. At the hour appointed the two set out, Pauline happily aware that she looked her very best. And why not? She had spent hours in getting ready and was wearing one of her prettiest dresses—a pale blue taffeta shot through with white—with blue silk shoes to match, and a large leghorn hat trimmed with pink rosebuds. Sparkling jewelry was at throat and wrists, and her dark curls fell becomingly to her shoulders.

"Darling, you do look lovely!" exclaimed Sophie as they entered the family carriage. "Oh, I'm so glad you're coming with me! And that you're all well again!"

Pauline shrugged. It was good to be well. And young and pretty. And yet—

"Dear Lord, if only this priest will say something to straighten me out," she thought. "Just any suggestion. . . ."

CHAPTER 4

THE FAMILY IS DISPLEASED

Father John Wurtz, a man of fifty-one, was not a dramatic speaker. Nevertheless, his simple sermon on vanity touched Pauline deeply, and she determined to have a few words with him as soon as Mass was over.

"He *is* a saint!" she thought. "I'm sure he'll be able to help me."

Of course Father Wurtz was a bit taken back to find a fashionably dressed young girl of sixteen seeking him out and attempting to explain how unhappy she was; how she loved the good things of life, and yet felt miserable even while she was enjoying them; how she believed God wanted something of her, but was afraid to think what it might be. And yet, unless she did find out soon, and did something about it, she would never know peace....

"Father, would you hear my confession, please, and then tell me what you think?" she begged impulsively.

With some reluctance (for he had had a long morning) Father Wurtz agreed. And soon he had promised to be Pauline's director, too. Yes, he would try to help in any way that he could—*if* Pauline would be honest with him and do what she was told.

"Father, I'll do anything you say!" exclaimed the girl eagerly. "Oh, if you just knew how I've been looking for a . . . a *real* friend!"

However, Pauline's happiness at finding someone who understood her particular problems was not exactly shared by the rest of the family. Of course it was good that she seemed to be happier and more content. But suddenly to spend so much time in prayer and works of charity! To sell several pieces of valuable jewelry in order to have more money to give to the poor! Surely this was going to extremes?

"Child, all you have to do is to ask me for any money you need," Anthony told her one day. "It's not at all necessary to sell your little trinkets."

Pauline nodded eagerly. "I know it's not, Papa. You're the most generous person in the world. You've always given me everything I want."

"Well, then—"

"But don't you see? You've given me too much! And it's kept me from hearing God's voice."

"*What?*"

"Yes, Papa. Father Wurtz says it's better for me to have only what's absolutely necessary." Then, as Anthony stared in anxious bewilderment: "But don't worry. I have so much jewelry that I don't know what to do with it. I'll never miss the pieces I sell."

For the time being, Anthony allowed himself to be persuaded. He even agreed that some of Pauline's silk and velvet evening gowns might be made into Mass vestments for poor churches. And the pretty flowers and ribbons which she had been accustomed to wear in her hair could be turned into wreaths for the little girls of the parish when they took part in religious processions. But when he presently discovered that his youngest daughter had spent the better part of a day with the incurable patients at Saint Polycarp's Hospital, waiting on them like a servant, washing them and dressing their sores, he was really worried.

"I don't like it," he told Paul and Phileas. "I think we'd better go and see this Father Wurtz before things get out of hand."

However, the two boys only laughed. "All this will never last," they said. "Why, you know Pauline, Papa! She's always been a great one for fads. It used to be with clothes. Now, she's taken up religion. But she'll be her old self again in a couple of weeks. Just wait and see."

But Pauline did not give up her new way of life. Every day she went to the incurable ward at Saint Polycarp's Hospital to do what she could for the poor people there. And noting that her pretty clothes set her apart from the other workers, she adopted a plainer mode of dress. The fashionable hats, with their feathers and flowers and lacy veils, gave place to the white muslin cap worn by factory girls; the flimsy shoes, with their fancy buckles and high heels, to sturdy wooden sandals with leather straps. And the dresses she selected for work were dark, plainly cut, and of a coarse and inexpensive material.

"Pauline Jaricot *is* losing her wits!" people told one another in amazement. "She didn't recover from that accident after all!"

"That's right. Why, she looks and acts just like a servant girl!"

"Ugh! And her hands! Have you noticed them? Stained and rough from all that horrible work at the hospital!"

"Really, someone ought to do something. Surely Sophie or Laurette could speak to her...."

"Or her father or brothers...."

Of course Pauline knew what her friends were saying, and her heart ached. How could she explain the reason for her present conduct? That she still loved nice things; that it was a real sacrifice to dress in ugly clothes; that even after considerable experience at the hospital, there were many times when she shrank from touching certain patients? And yet, surely all this sacrifice was necessary. It was a kind of purification, so to speak, so that some day, somehow, she might be able to hear the voice of God and take up the work which He had prepared for her from all eternity....

"Because He *does* have some kind of work for me to do," Pauline told herself over and over again. "I'm sure of that."

Yet her heart continued to be troubled. If only Mama were still alive! She would understand this new way of life—and why it had been necessary to break so completely with the old. But Mama was gone. And there was really no one to whom to turn.

"Dear Lord, couldn't You please hurry and tell me what it is that You want of me?" was the girl's constant prayer. "I'm so alone!"

The days passed, however, and seemingly there was no answer to Pauline's request. Many times, lonely and discouraged, she locked herself in her room and gazed sadly at the few attractive dresses still remaining in her wardrobe. Pale blue, green, yellow, pink—how pretty they were! And how easy it would be to slip into one of them and take up the old way of life again! But they were only for special occasions—such as Sundays and feast days—when, in order not to embarrass the family, she dressed as in the old days and went with them to High Mass in the parish church.

Then one day Pauline came to a painful decision. For a whole year she would wear nothing but purple, the color she hated most. And the next time she went to High Mass, her dress would be patterned after one of the plain and ugly ones she wore to work at the hospital.

"Now, Lord, with this new sacrifice, will You tell me what You want of me?" she asked.

CHAPTER 5

THINGS BEGIN TO GET CLEAR

Poor Pauline! She was a girl of moods, and when Sunday came she was almost in despair. How could she walk up the center aisle of the parish church, the eyes of the fashionable congregation upon her, in a dress that was no better than that of a girl working in her father's silk factory? And purple at that!

"I . . . I can't do it!" she muttered. "It was a foolish promise."

"*No,*" said a little voice in her heart, "*it was a good promise, Pauline. Hurry up now, or you'll be late.*"

"But everyone will stare at me. And laugh, too."

"*What of that?*"

"I . . . I don't like being laughed at."

"*Of course not. Nobody does. But think of the merit such a sacrifice will bring! And remember, God expects a good many sacrifices before He's ready to explain about the great work He has in store for you.*"

"Well, I'll make some other sacrifice—I'll do anything else."

"*No, this is the one He wants.*"

"B-but—"

"That's enough, Pauline. Hurry up now, and get ready for church."

Trembling, and on the verge of tears, Pauline found one of her new purple dresses and put it on. How ugly it was, even with a white kerchief about the shoulders to relieve the drabness! As for the clumsy wooden sandals on her feet, the coarse muslin cap of a working girl which all but hid her pretty curls. . .

"Dear Lord, help me!" she choked. *"Help me!"*

Presently, shaking in every limb, Pauline was making her way up the center aisle of the parish church. All heads turned at the sound of her clattering sandals, and there was a gasp of astonishment among the fashionably dressed congregation. Of course several had already seen Pauline's new work-a-day garb, but no one had ever dreamed she would appear in it at Sunday Mass.

"The poor girl *is* out of her mind," whispered one woman compassionately. "I knew it right along."

Pauline's cheeks burned as she stumbled into a pew and tried to collect her thoughts. What a terrible, terrible day! And how awful for the family, too! There was none of the peace one sometimes has in doing a difficult thing one knows is right. She felt sick with shame. And yet, if she was to break with the old life, half-measures would never do.

"Lord, tell me what You want of me!" she begged silently. "And give me the strength to say 'yes'!"

The prayer was not answered right away. Indeed, for several weeks Pauline had still to go on with her work at the hospital, braving the criticism of both family and friends, with none of the peace of mind she had hoped for. Many times she was

"THE POOR GIRL'S OUT OF HER MIND!"

almost on the point of breaking down where clothes were concerned. After all, there was nothing wrong in having good taste and using it. But whenever she was tempted to finger the few pretty dresses remaining in her wardrobe, the matching hats and shoes, the really lovely jewelry which the family had given her, a counsel of Saint Francis de Sales echoed warningly in her ears: *If you do not wish to sell your wares, lower the signboard.*

It was enough for Pauline. Gone were the days when she had tried to sell herself by being the center of attraction in her own little circle. Approval, admiration, the friendship of others, were still heart-warming things, of course, but she could live without them. In fact, she *must.* It was the price which God had set upon the mysterious work He wanted her to do. But oh, how long it was taking Him to let her know what this was!

"Lord, please hurry!" she prayed. "I don't trust myself. . . ."

Then one day while on a visit to her married sister Laurette (who lived at nearby Saint-Vallier), Pauline felt herself on the verge of a comforting discovery. Suppose she was meant to do something for the workers in her brother-in-law's silk factory? The Jaricot fortune had been built on the labors of just such people, and it seemed only right that someone in the family should take a personal interest in their welfare.

"Laurette, do you think Victor would mind if I went to his factory and tried to make friends with the girls there?" she asked hopefully. "I . . . I'd like to help them if I could."

Twenty-five-year-old Laurette Chartron hesitated. Like everyone else, she had never lost hope that Pauline would give up her old ways and some day make a good marriage. Still—

"Darling, you know Victor would love to have you visit the factory whenever you want to," she said finally. "But— well, what could you possibly do for the girls? We pay them good wages, and they seem happy enough."

Pauline nodded. "I know. Yet they must have troubles. And if they could just talk to someone, especially to one of us Jaricots... if they could feel we were friends as well as employers...."

Victor Chartron agreed that Pauline's suggestion was a good one. With considerable political unrest in and about Lyons, a poor harvest and rising food prices, the lot of the working man was a hard one. Spirits were frequently low, even among his own well-paid employees, and if Pauline could bring just a little comfort to the two hundred girls working at the factory—

"Go ahead, my dear," he said kindly. "Do whatever you think best."

So Pauline became a regular visitor at the Chartron silk factory. At first the girls eyed her distrustfully as she came among them at their looms and replied only briefly to her questions. After all, even though she dressed as plainly as themselves, Mademoiselle Jaricot did belong to another world. How could she possibly care what they did after work, where and how they lived, whether there was sickness or other trouble at home?

"She's up to no good," some declared suspiciously.

"She's been queer ever since she was hurt," others announced.

But Pauline did not give up hope, and after some weeks a number of the girls had become her loyal friends. In fact, they were constantly singing her praises—how she assisted at

four o'clock Mass every morning, gave food, money and clothing to anyone in need, not only at the factory but at the
hospitals, too. Then, how pretty she was, despite her unattrac-
tive clothes! How kind and understanding! It was a pleasure
to talk to her.

Naturally Pauline was grateful for the success of her
venture, and especially that Father Wurtz had given it his
wholehearted approval. According to him, the working class
had been drifting away from the Church for years. Now,
how splendid that at last someone was taking a friendly interest in their welfare! Certainly it did little good to preach the
Word of God to people who where hungry, poorly-housed and
resentful of their lot in life. If they listened at all, it was
only with tongue in cheek. And though the workers at the
Chartron factory were well treated and better paid than most,
they nevertheless shared the attitude of a class which had
suffered long from injustice and had little hope of the per-
manency of any improvement in their circumstances. But if
Pauline and others like her were to go among them, win their
confidence and try to better their lot—

"This *may* be the task God has in store for you, child,"
he agreed thoughtfully, "to bring the workers back to Christ."

Pauline's eyes shone. "Oh, Father, how I hope so!" she
exclaimed. "After all, my family and I do owe these people
so much. . . ."

Surprisingly enough, Pauline's twenty-year-old brother Phileas was extremely interested in her new venture. No longer
did he tease his young sister about her "conversion." In fact,
he was beginning to turn over a new leaf himself. Suddenly
he seemed to have tired of being a rich man's son, with nothing

to do but amuse himself. He had now taken to hearing Mass daily, reading spiritual books, visiting the sick poor and those in prison, and dispensing alms with a generous hand.

"The spirit must be catching," was the general verdict. "First Pauline, now Phileas. What's going to happen next?"

Anthony Jaricot was as puzzled as anyone else. Could Phileas be developing a vocation to the priesthood? Was eighteen-year-old Pauline also considering giving herself to God in the religious life? Or had these two youngest of his five living children decided to spend their days in being—well, *different?*

"If only Joan were alive!" he sighed. "She'd know what to do."

But Joan Jaricot had been dead for three years, and in the end it was Father Wurtz to whom Anthony went for advice and consolation.

"Don't worry, sir," said the priest kindly. "I'm sure the Lord has some great work in store for both Phileas and Pauline."

Anthony shook his head doubtfully. "But what, Father? I know it's a fine thing to be interested in the poor. And I've never refused to let my children be as charitable as they wished. But when a man's built up a fine business such as mine, and finds himself growing old, it's only natural for him to try to do something about keeping it in the family."

"Of course, sir. But won't Paul see to that?"

"How can he? His Julie died after only a year of marriage, and there are no children. Besides, I always did count on the younger boy. . . ."

Poor Anthony Jaricot! Despite the reassuring words of Father Wurtz, he grew more and more depressed as the days passed. Sophie and Laurette were happily married, of course. Eventually Paul might find himself a second wife. But Phileas and Pauline, upon whom he had built such hopes—

"Maybe I'd better get some prayers," he decided finally, his thoughts turning to Father Charles Balley, the sixty-six-year-old pastor of nearby Ecully. This good priest, in the company of Father John Vianney, his thirty-one-year-old assistant, had often visited at Tassin, the Jaricot country house, and Anthony had always taken pleasure in sending them home with a generous alms. But now rumor had it that Father Balley's traveling days were over. He had fallen victim to a painful leg infection, and it was doubtful whether he would live through the year.

"The man's a saint," Anthony reflected. "If I can get just a few prayers from him, in the midst of that great suffering, surely everything will turn out well for all of us?"

CHAPTER 6

MISSION PROJECTS

Sophie and Laurette joined their father in his hopes that Phileas and Pauline might soon settle down to a more regular way of life. But the year 1818 brought no answer to their prayers. Instead, both brother and sister continued to work among the underprivileged of Lyons, heedless of all criticism. As for Father Charles Balley, he had finally succumbed to his illness, and his young assistant was now pastor in the obscure little village of Ars. Here, from all accounts, he was very busy. At any rate, he no longer paid social calls to Tassin.

"Never mind, Papa," said the two girls. "As Mama used to say: 'All this is the Will of God.' And you must admit that Phileas and Pauline seem much happier than in the old days."

Anthony hesitated. "Y-yes," he agreed finally. "I suppose so."

"Sir, you *know* it's so!" protested Zachary Perrin, Sophie's husband. "And as far as Pauline is concerned, I'm not in the least surprised. Why, what that girl has accomplished at Saint-Vallier is little short of a miracle!" And he began to relate all that his young sister-in-law had done at the Chartron factory—how she had made personal friends of the two hundred girls working there, so that now they invariably came to her with their problems; how she had even brought several back to their religious duties, and had also made it a point for everyone to stop work at three o'clock each afternoon to recite three Our Fathers and three Hail Marys in honor of Our Lord's death upon the Cross. According to Victor Chartron, the spirit in his workrooms was at a higher level than it had ever been before.

"Pauline's formed some kind of a society, too, sir—the Reparatrices of the Heart of Jesus," continued Zachary enthusiastically. "She and a few of the girls make the Way of the Cross each day, and pray for the return of France to the Faith."

In spite of himself, a smile crossed Anthony's troubled face. He was well aware of all that Pauline was doing, of course, but it was good to hear about it from others, too.

"Bless the child!" he murmured. "She always did know how to organize."

However, it was not only at Saint-Vallier that nineteen-year-old Pauline had endeared herself to the workers. By now she had also made her influence felt in Lyons, persuading several men and women at the Jaricot silk factory to join her in praying for the return of France to the Faith. And on the suggestion of Phileas, there were also prayers and a weekly collection of a penny each for the benefit of the foreign missions. Of course the amount collected was small, but no one worried about that. In China, less than thirty-seven dollars would support a catechist or lay instructor for a whole year.

"Certain Protestant groups in England have adopted such

a plan of giving a penny a week for their missions," Phileas
had explained to Pauline. "I read about it just recently. Now
if they're so anxious to spread error, why should we hesitate
to spread truth?"

Pauline received the suggestion with joy. What a wonderful idea! And how clever of Phileas to have thought of it!

"We'll start right in," she announced eagerly. "Even the
poorest people can afford a penny a week."

Pauline's loyal followers among the Reparatrices agreed.
Not only was Phileas' plan a practical one, as far as the
foreign missions were concerned. It would be a wonderful
help in explaining the doctrine of the Mystical Body of Christ
to the workers. Until now, partly because of the pressure of
their poverty, partly because of a lack of instruction, they had
thought of themselves chiefly as individuals struggling to make
a living. They had never thought of themselves as members
in the Body of the Church, sharing in the merit gained by
other members and able to give their own share for the good
of all—a share that might be as important, or more important,
than that of the Pope himself. No one had ever told them
that a penny offered to help the spread of the True Faith
in China would do far more than benefit an unknown pagan.
It would actually increase the sum total of merit in the Church's
treasury upon which they themselves, in time of need, would
be entitled to draw.

"Yes, that's the way it is," Pauline agreed enthusiastically.
"Every time a pagan is baptized, our whole Christian family
becomes stronger and richer."

Soon additional factory hands at Saint-Vallier and Lyons
were bringing their pennies to Pauline. How wonderful that

their tiny offerings could be of such value! Why, the mere thought could make one feel good for a whole day! As for Phileas, who was temporarily charged with distributing the funds to the proper authorities, he was greatly encouraged. Already there was more than enough to support a catechist in China for the better part of a year. And statistics showed that a catechist often baptized more than two thousand abandoned children in the course of his lifetime, not to mention several hundred adults.

Pauline's spirits soared. Could it be possible that just four years ago she had been a hopeless invalid, convinced that life held nothing for her but pain and discouragement? Now, each day was far too short for all the work there was to be done.

"Dear Lord, thank You for everything!" was her constant prayer. "And especially for letting me be useful!"

Then in the spring of 1819 there was fresh cause for rejoicing when Phileas announced his intention of studying for the priesthood. God willing, he would be ordained within four years and spend his life as a missionary in China.

The Reparatrices of the Heart of Jesus were as proud and pleased as Pauline. It might well be, they told one another hopefully, that their prayers and sacrifices had helped to win this priestly vocation. At any rate, it was surely a sign that God was pleased with their work, and so they renewed their efforts to interest friends and families in the missions, as well as to read a devotional booklet published by the Foreign Mission Society in Paris.

This booklet had a rather long title: *Association of Prayers to Ask of God the Conversion of Pagans, the Perseverance of*

Christians who Live in the Midst of Them, and the Prosperity of Establishments Working for the Propagation of the Faith. However, it had long since been popularly shortened to *The Propagation of the Faith,* a title which the Reparatrices presently applied to their own work.

Pauline was thoroughly familiar with the booklet, too, and made all the religious practices suggested in it her own. Thus, each day she recited the *Memorare* and a prayer to Saint Francis Xavier for the success of the foreign missions. Also, every Friday was given over to various good works for the conversion of the heathen. But busy as she was with her many projects, she did not forget the wise counsel of Father Wurtz. Every day she must spend some time before the Blessed Sacrament. Here she need say no special prayers, only give herself up to silent adoration on her knees. Of course some people might think all this a waste of time, but it was not so.

"God doesn't really *need* His creatures or their works," the priest had explained. "Not even such a good work as the Propagation of the Faith. But when we come to visit Him in childlike confidence, His Heart is touched. Then it is that He showers upon us infinite blessings. Sometimes we are conscious of these benefits and go away encouraged. More often than not we feel nothing, and go away more lonely than before. But this doesn't matter, child. Our Lord in the Blessed Sacrament always has some grace for those who come to visit Him. In this life we may never recognize it for what it is, but it is real just the same."

So every day Pauline made at least one visit to the Blessed Sacrament. Sometimes she found it very easy to pour out her love and gratitude for all the Lord was doing for her. At others, she could only look at the Tabernacle in hurt bewilderment. Things had not been going at all well. Although she still wanted to do God's Will, the way of life she had taken upon herself was surely too much. Try though she would, there were patients at the hospitals whom she could scarcely bear to touch. Then, her friends of former days! How next to impossible not to be envious of their pretty clothes when she passed them in the street and felt their scornful, amused or even pitying glances! Truly, it would be far easier to run away and bury herself in a convent than to walk about Lyons in the cheap and hateful garb she was making herself wear. And when she remembered that her sense of fashion far excelled that of these same friends; that she could give so much pleasure to her family by dressing as in the old days. . . .

Pauline's acts of faith in God's Providence were many as she knelt before the Blessed Sacrament during the year 1819. However, on occasion there were consolations, too, when she seemed to hear a voice in her heart promising that all would be well. Once in particular, as she knelt with closed eyes before the Tabernacle, she had such an extraordinary experience that she felt impelled to describe it to her friends among the Reparatrices when they came to the Jaricot house for their regular weekly meeting.

"I seemed to see two oil lamps," she told them, "one full, the other empty. And as I watched, the empty one began to fill itself from the full one. Suddenly I knew the empty lamp represented Europe, which has been losing the Faith for so long. But—well, what do you think the full lamp stood for?"

The Reparatrices shook their heads. "What?" asked one girl doubtfully.

Pauline took a deep breath. "The full lamp represented the pagan countries of the world!" she declared triumphantly. "I'm sure of that. Oh, don't you see what this means? Some day Europe, and France especially, will regain the Faith through the prayers and good works of the converts it makes in foreign countries!"

Pauline's conviction was so evident that the girls could not help but share it. What a thought—that the pennies they were collecting could do so much! Certainly they must renew their efforts to gather more and more. As for Pauline, it had been in her mind for some time that friends in other cities— Nancy, Metz, Havre, Rennes—might also like to help the missions by offering a penny each week and reciting the prayers suggested in the booklet published by the Foreign Mission Society in Paris.

"I'll write to them right way," she decided. "And I'll ask Phileas to do the same."

CHAPTER 7

THE NEW PLAN—WORKING TOO WELL?

There was little difficulty in establishing the desired groups, and presently Pauline was able to send still larger amounts to her brother for distribution among the missionaries in China. However, one vexing problem remained. The practical side of the work had never been properly organized, and frequently (because of sickness, forgetfulness, or for other reasons) those who had promised to contribute a penny a week failed to make their returns.

"There ought to be some kind of plan to offset all this," Pauline told herself. "The way things are, there's too much left to chance."

Phileas had only one suggestion. Why didn't Pauline pray especially hard for enlightenment? The fact that the Propagation of the Faith had sprung into being so spontaneously, and was so unpretentious a movement (after all, what could be less imposing than the pennies of the poor?) was nothing to worry about. Humanly speaking, of course, the venture could never amount to much. However, God frequently used the weak things of this world for His own ends, and made them prosper. Whereas other worthy causes, relying solely upon worldly strength and riches—

"Go ahead," he wrote. "If you pray much, if you listen humbly and lovingly to the voice of the Sacred Heart of Jesus, He will perhaps inspire you with a plan."

So Pauline began to pray. Surely there must be some way to simplify her work for the missions, to guarantee that the pennies of the poor would come in regularly and find their way to China?

Sophie and Laurette were doubtful. As for Anthony, he did not know what to think. Of course it was good to see Pauline her old self again, busy and eager and aglow with high spirits. But she was no longer his little girl, he told himself sadly. She belonged to too many other people now, and the house was always full of strangers—hungry, fretful, sick or unemployed—waiting to consult her about their problems.

"The worst of it is, she seems to *like* being with these wretched people," he mourned, recalling those far-off days when the sole aim of his youngest daughter had been to be the best-dressed and most popular girl in Lyons. Now, in her unbecoming purple clothes, clumsy wooden sandals on her feet, her hands rough and stained from hours spent in working at the hospitals—

"It's not right," he reflected uneasily. "The poor child should be thinking about her own future. As for her old father, I'm afraid she's forgotten all about him."

Pauline only laughed at such notions. "Papa, you *know* I love you—better than anyone else in the whole world!" she protested gaily. "And why shouldn't I, when you've always been so kind and generous?" Then, with a reassuring hug and kiss: "And God loves you, too, for all the wonderful things you've done for His poor."

"But—"

"And isn't it splendid, Papa, that we've got so many people interested in the missions? Why, if things keep on like this, we'll soon be supporting ten catechists in China!"

In spite of himself, Anthony smiled. His little girl *was* happy. And she did love him. What more could he ask?

Despite her gay air, however, Pauline sensed the pathos of the situation. Her father was desperately lonely. The death of his wife five years ago had left a void in his heart which nothing had been able to fill. Formerly his prosperous silk factory had claimed his full attention, but the one fortune he already had made was enough for Anthony Jaricot. Now, in his middle sixties, he had less and less interest in business matters.

"Poor Papa, he just wants his children about him," Pauline reflected. "And here we are, scattered in this place and that, busy with our own affairs."

Since she was the only one left at home, Pauline decided to do what she could to make life more pleasant for her father. Accordingly, she tried to set aside an hour or so each day to read to him, or just to talk. Paul, traveling in Italy, and Phileas, studying at the Seminary, also realized how things were, and wrote frequently. As for Sophie and Laurette, they made it a point to visit the Jaricot house as often as they could, and to bring their children with them.

One evening, when Sophie and her husband had been guests for dinner, Pauline observed with pleasure how relaxed and happy her father was looking. The family had just come into the drawing room and was settling down for a game of cards. She had been invited to play, too, but had asked to be excused because of her cold. However, from her place before the cheerful fire, she could hear the talk and laughter of the others.

"Dear God, thank You!" she murmured contentedly. "You *have* been good. . . ."

For the better part of an hour Pauline continued to sit drowsily before the glowing embers. Thoughts of her mother came to her mind, and she prayed for the repose of her soul. She remembered Narcissus, too, the sickly twenty-year-old brother who had died one year before his mother. And then John Marie, that other brother who had gone home to God when scarcely six years old, long before she herself had been born—

"May they all rest in peace," she whispered.

Presently she roused herself to think about the problem uppermost in her mind. What was to be done about placing the Propagation of the Faith on a sounder basis? She had prayed long and earnestly to the Sacred Heart about this, as Phileas had suggested, but as yet no solution had presented itself. Still, there must be some way in which to guarantee that the mission pennies should be collected each week without fail. After all, in the Chartron factory alone there were dozens of girls who had promised to give this amount for the support of the Church in China and were willing to keep their word. Then there were the groups in Lyons, too, as well as those recently started in other cities. But the whole set-up was so loose and unwieldy that people forgot, and already a number of would-be donors had been lost track of—

"Lord, what are we going to do?" demanded Pauline earnestly.

Then suddenly she sat bolt upright. A plan had occurred to her, so amazingly simple that she wondered why she had never thought of it before. Instead of having an indefinite number of friends sending in their weekly pennies only when they remembered to do so, she would ask them to band into groups of ten, with one member in each group assigned to act as collector. When ten such groups had been formed, the collectors would turn over their individual returns to a leader. And if the work should prosper to such an extent that one thousand people were making contributions, there would be still another person to take charge of this larger unit.

"Groups of ten, groups of a hundred, groups of a thousand —each with their own leader!" thought Pauline excitedly. "Dear Lord, I do believe this is it!"

Eager to see the plan worked out on paper, she borrowed a score sheet from the card table and jotted down details. God willing, she would discuss everything with Father Wurtz as soon as possible. However, since he was now living at some distance from the city, she had better consult first with her own pastor, Father Guichardot. Experienced as he was in business matters, he would surely know whether the plan was practical or not.

"After all, there could be some flaw in it," she admitted uneasily.

But the next day, to Pauline's relief, Father Guichardot declared that the plan was splendid, and should be put into effect at once. And when she finally succeeded in explaining matters to Father Wurtz, he also was enthusiastic.

"Pauline, you couldn't possibly have come upon this scheme

"I DO BELIEVE THIS IS IT!"

44

all by yourself," he declared. "It's inspired by God. Go ahead and carry it out with my blessing."

Pauline lost no time in doing just this, and in a few weeks the pennies were pouring in as never before. The new scheme for aiding the foreign missions was being accepted with enthusiasm, and additional groups of tens were being formed with scarcely any trouble. This was largely due to the suggestion that from now on every contributor to the Propagation of the Faith should try to form his own group of ten, stressing especially the importance to everyone of a strong and vital Catholic group in China.

"Remember Pauline's story about the two oil lamps," one person told another. "It could be that the prayers and good works of our Chinese brothers will restore the Faith to France and to the rest of Europe as well."

For several weeks the work continued to prosper. Then came unexpected trouble. A priest from a neighboring parish called to inform Pauline that a girl of twenty had no right to be handling large sums of money belonging to the Church. She had forgotten her place, and it was high time someone told her so.

"Besides, have you permission from the Cardinal Archbishop for what you're doing?" he demanded suspiciously.

Pauline's heart sank as she gazed at her visitor. "Why, no, Father," she admitted. "His Eminence is in Rome, you know, and I never once thought—"

The priest's face was stern. "Well, you'd better start to think, young lady," he warned. "All this collecting of money by an unauthorized lay person is most irregular."

CHAPTER 8

MORE OBSTACLES CROP UP

Poor Pauline! It had never occurred to her that the permission of her pastor and that of her director were not sufficient for the work she had undertaken to do. And since the Cardinal Archbishop of Lyons had gone to live in Rome because of various political troubles in France, there was no hope of discussing matters with him. Still, he had appointed three Vicars General to administer the affairs of the archdiocese in his absence. . . .

"I'll write to one of them and apologize for everything," she decided. "Perhaps to Monsignor Courbon. Surely he'll understand and give us his blessing."

However, the Monsignor's reply to Pauline's letter was less than cordial. There was no need to stop the present work, he said, but under no circumstances must it be allowed to expand.

"Why, that was our only hope of success!" Pauline told herself in dismay. "More and more groups of tens, of hundreds, of thousands! More and more pennies for China! But this way. . . ."

Greatly perplexed, she decided to consult Monsignor Gourdiat, who had recently replaced Father Guichardot as pastor of her parish. Perhaps he might have some suggestions. And since he was also a Vicar General, his word would carry equal weight with that of Monsignor Courbon.

"Dear God, what a fool I've been!" she thought as she prepared for the interview. "If anything happens to spoil things now, it'll be all my fault."

However, Monsignor Gourdiat was very kind. "By all means go ahead with the work," he said encouragingly. "Collect all the money you can and bring it to me. I'll see that it reaches the Foreign Mission Society in Paris." Then, with a smile: "And I'll also explain matters to Monsignor Courbon."

But as reviving confidence revealed itself in Pauline's eyes, the Monsignor shook a finger in warning. "One thing more, child. This little taste of trouble you've just had—of course you know why it came?"

Pauline nodded eagerly. "Oh, yes, Monsignor. It's because I was so thoughtless. I should have remembered that His Eminence—"

"No, no, that's only part of the story. You've had this trouble because your work is turning out so well. At first, when it was only small, the Devil never bothered about it. But now that you've organized things so skillfully that hundreds of people are becoming mission-minded—well, things are taking a different turn. The Evil One's decided to stir up some misunderstanding. Later on he'll probably be up to other mischief, too, just to discourage you."

Pauline stared. "But Monsignor! Why in the world...."

"My dear, be prepared for what I tell you. Suffering always accompanies any worthwhile work. The sooner you learn that, and—relying upon God's Providence—accept it cheerfully, the better off you'll be."

As the weeks passed, Pauline had frequent occasion to discover the truth in Monsignor Gourdiat's words. Certain people whom she had always admired and trusted began to show traits she had never known existed in them. They accused her of being proud and eager for publicity, not for the good of the missions but for her own private ends. She was involved in a work which should be handled by a priest, they said. After all, hadn't her own great patron, Saint Paul the Apostle, cautioned against women taking too prominent a part in Church affairs? It would be far better if she kept in the background and minded her own business.

At first Pauline was shocked and hurt. Well she knew that she was only a tool in God's hands; that, in His goodness, He had chosen to give her the necessary strength and intelligence to organize an important work for Him, rather than pass her days as a helpless invalid. But when idle tongues began to suggest that she was still not really herself mentally (because of the accident which had happened five years ago); that no wealthy young woman in her right mind would dress so unbecomingly and spurn all offers of marriage, her temper flared.

"It's not so!" she protested to Victor Girodon when she heard of the gossip. "I *am* in my right mind! And I *won't* stop helping the missions! Why, I'm willing to die for the work if necessary!"

Pauline's friends among the Reparatrices had been quick to come to her defense, but among her staunchest supporters was this young man who had become interested in the work in its early days.

"Don't mind this nasty talk, Pauline," he said kindly. "Apparently some people here in Lyons can't bear to think that it was a girl of twenty who put the Propagation of the Faith on a sound basis. They wish they'd thought of your plan themselves—the collecting by tens and hundreds and thousands."

Pauline swallowed hard. What a comfort Victor was! An inspector in one of the city's largest silk mills, he had succeeded in recruiting even more workers for the missions than she had. In fact, he was now in charge of all the donations made by men, while she looked after those of the women. At stated intervals the joint returns were given to Monsignor Gourdiat to forward to the Foreign Mission Society in Paris.

"I . . . I'm sorry, Victor," she choked. "I shouldn't lose my temper like that. It's very childish."

Victor smiled. He admired Pauline immensely, and Phileas, too. And it was a source of comfort to remember that both were praying that some day soon he would be able to enter the Seminary and study for the priesthood.

"Don't apologize," he said sympathetically. "I'd be furious if I were in your place."

Despite the jealous and malicious gossip, Pauline continued her work with the Propagation of the Faith. She also began another project among those of the upper class in Lyons who were still impoverished from the Revolution of thirty-one years ago. The girls and women of this group, never taught to make a living, were yet reluctant to accept charity. Pauline offered to teach them how to make artificial flowers from bits of silk and velvet from the Jaricot factory, and to market their wares as well. A workroom was opened (with funds supplied by Anthony), which soon became self-supporting. However, it was still the foreign missions which claimed Pauline's chief attention. *And* the return to the Faith of the French working class. For these two intentions, she and her Reparatrices continued to make the Way of the Cross each day and to visit the Blessed Sacrament as frequently as possible.

Sophie and Laurette were troubled. How much their young sister had taken upon herself! Each day began with Mass at four o'clock. Her mornings were evenly divided between clerical work for the Propagation of the Faith and caring for the sick at the hospitals. In the afternoons she was to be found either visiting the poor in their homes or those in prison who were sick or dying. Of course she did give the evening hours to her father, reading to him or playing cards. But, reported Rose, the faithful Jaricot maid, when Monsieur Jaricot had gone to bed, Mademoiselle Pauline shut herself up in her room to pray, instead of taking her own much-needed rest.

"It's not right," Sophie and Laurette told each other anxiously. "Pauline's young, yes. Only twenty-two. But even so, she'll lose her health if she keeps on like this."

Pauline only laughed at her sisters' fears. "I feel fine," she told them gaily. "And I get far more rest than you think." But one day, alarmed by her pallor and shortness of breath, Anthony called a doctor and insisted upon a thorough examination. As a result, Pauline was ordered to bed at once. She had a bad heart, a weakness in one lung, and several other ailments, said the doctor. A six months' rest was absolutely necessary, and even then she would be far from well.

Much against her wishes, Pauline did as she was told. As for the Reparatrices in Saint-Vallier and Lyons, they began to storm heaven for her cure. How dismal life would be if she were taken from them! Why, they had never known such a wonderful friend before!

"We'll do everything possible to help her," they decided. "No sacrifice will be too great."

The doctor only shook his head when he heard of the prayers and good works that were being offered for Pauline's recovery. However, in just one week he was forced to admit that she was improving. And when a month had passed and she was up and around and as busy as usual, he was beside himself with amazement.

"I don't understand it," he said. "Why, according to all the rules, that girl should be an invalid for a year or more!"

Of course Pauline was delighted to be back at work again. Despite the continued opposition of a few enemies, the Propagation of the Faith was flourishing as never before, and her heart sang at the thought of all the good that was being accomplished in China. However, in the spring of 1822 there were unexpected difficulties. A certain Father Inglesi arrived in Lyons as the representative of Bishop Dubourg of New Orleans to ask for help for the missions in America. While admitting that the priests in China could use all the pennies sent to them, he pointed out that America was a missionary country, too, and in dire need of aid. Surely the Propagation of the Faith could take up a second collection to help support the Church in the New World?

Pauline hesitated. It would be a wonderful thing to help the Church in America. The Sulpician Fathers, who were already working there, were suffering incredible hardships because of lack of funds. On the other hand, although it was certainly prospering, the Propagation of the Faith was scarcely three years old. . . .

"Father, I'm afraid we aren't big enough yet to support two separate charities," she said respectfully. "Besides, we've told all our friends that their pennies are being used for the Church in China. It would only confuse them if we changed things now."

"Yes," put in Victor Girodon. "And worse than that, Father. If we did have two collections, we might not be able to get enough to help either the Church in China or the Church in America to any real extent."

Father Inglesi was unimpressed. "My young friends, you just don't understand," he said impatiently. "The Propagation of the Faith can do wonderful things if you'll only give it a chance. Now, suppose you let me tell you what I have in mind."

Pauline and Victor exchanged furtive glances. Try though they would to ignore it, there was something disturbing about this strange priest. Of course he had a wonderful eloquence, and many important people were now his friends, including King Louis the Eighteenth. And yet—

"Well," demanded Father Inglesi in hurt tones, seeing that the two young people before him had all but ignored his offer, "don't you want to hear what I have to say?"

With an effort, Pauline managed an apologetic smile. "Forgive us, Father," she said hastily. "Of course we do."

"Yes, yes," agreed Victor, not wishing to appear rude. "We know a little about America, of course. But it'd be a pleasure to hear more from you, Father. Especially about your own work."

CHAPTER 9

GROWING PAINS

Soon Father Inglesi was talking enthusiastically about the American missions. There was no worthier cause that the Propagation of the Faith could adopt, he insisted. After all, · the future of Europe was far more closely connected with the New World than it was with Asia. Wouldn't it be better to establish a strong Catholic group in America, rather than in a backward land like China? Such an investment would pay wonderful dividends, and in a short time.

Pauline and Victor listened in troubled silence. Certainly Father Inglesi had a marvelous skill with words. The picture he painted of the vast stretches of American wilderness peopled with Indians who had never heard the Word of God, the dreadful hardships of the few missionaries who were trying to work among them, was fascinating. But when they were again alone, the spell began to break. Of course America would have a great future. Even now people from many parts of Europe, especially England and France, were going there to settle. And yet—

"China's important, too," they decided. "We just can't forget about the millions of pagans there."

But Father Inglesi was not to be discouraged. Within a short time he had talked to so many in Lyons about the American missions that several members of the Propagation of the Faith were won over to his side. However, one important leader named Benedict Coste agreed with Pauline and Victor that it would be most unwise to take up the second collection Father Inglesi had suggested.

"If we do that, somebody else will come along with another worthy cause, then another and another," he said. "We'll end up with dozens of small charities on our hands, and not be able to help any of them properly."

Pauline nodded vigorously. "That's just what I've been saying right along," she declared. "And Victor, too."

For a moment Benedict was thoughtful. "Still, there *is* one solution," he remarked finally. "We might reorganize and make ourselves into a worldwide group. Then we could help everybody."

Pauline stared. A worldwide group? Surely that was asking for too much! Up until now the Propagation of the Faith had succeeded because it was a small and compact affair. Large donations, although welcome, had never been sought, only the pennies of the poor. But now—

"I . . . I don't think a plan like that would work," she said hesitantly. "At least, not just yet."

"Neither do I," confessed Victor. "We'd do better to be satisfied with the way things are."

But in just a few weeks both young people sensed that a change was unavoidable. By now Father Inglesi's forceful personality had won him even more friends, and interest in the American missions was increasing on every side. On May 3 a meeting was held to discuss the advisability of sending some

financial aid to Bishop Dubourg of New Orleans as a gesture
of friendship. However, Benedicte Coste managed to hold his
ground. Either the Propagation of the Faith ought to remain
as it was—a small, compact affair to help the Church in China
—or it should be reorganized to include the missions of the
whole world. There was no point in trying to have a number
of collections for whatever worthy cause might strike a member's fancy.

Pauline did not attend the meeting and took scarcely any
part in the ensuing argument. And when a second meeting
was held on May 25, at which time it was decided to adopt
the plan of Benedict Coste, she did little more than promise
her support. After all, the whole affair was so breathtaking!
A worldwide plan to help the missions was wonderful, of
course. But would it succeed? Centers would have to be
created all over Europe, committees formed, then sub-com-
mittees. . . .

"It's so *big!*" she thought.

But Victor Girodon was beginning to be convinced of the
worth of the new set-up, and reassured her. Wasn't Benedict
Coste one of their best workers, a practical and religious man
who knew what he was doing? The same was true of others
among the laity and clergy who were to take over important
positions. And since Pauline's original scheme of collecting
pennies from groups of tens and hundreds and thousands would
still be followed, there was no need to worry about the work
being taken away from the poor, or of its having a new form.

"I'm turning over my list of names to the new committee
right away," declared Victor enthusiastically. "You'll do the
same, won't you?"

Pauline hesitated, then nodded slowly. "Yes," she said. "I suppose that's the only thing to do."

But even as she spoke, resentment stirred faintly within her. Of course the new committee was out to do a great work. And the members had already proved themselves loyal and zealous friends of the missions. But they *had* overridden her wishes. They *had* let themselves be influenced by Father Inglesi. Now the humble little project which she had started three years ago among the Reparatrices at Saint-Vallier and in Lyons was being taken over by others. . . .

"No, no that's ridiculous!" she told herself sharply. "You're just jealous, Pauline." And stifling her feelings as best she could, she determined to hand over the names of those of her friends who could be counted upon to contribute a penny a week for the missions.

By September of that same year, 1822, under the guidance of the new and energetic committee, the work of the Society for the Propagation of the Faith had assumed such proportions that it was decided to have two central offices—one in Lyons and the other in Paris. In March, 1823, Pope Pius the Seventh sent his blessing, whereupon public interest in the group reached new heights. Additional members were recruited from all over France, impressed by two important features: the simplicity of the cause and its immense possibilities. Even a child could perform the two good works required for membership—the daily recitation of one Our Father, Hail Mary and the ejaculation, *Saint Francis Xavier, pray for us,* plus the contribution of a penny a week.

"We should have had something like this long ago," one person told another.

"PLEASE WORK WITH US, PAULINE!"

"That's right. Although we've never realized it, the foreign missions belong to us as much as to the missionaries."

"Of course. But not only the responsibility. There's also a big reward for helping to bring the Faith to others."

"Yes. Every time a pagan is baptized, the entire Christian family benefits."

"You mean it becomes holier and happier because we all have the chance to share in our new brother's good works?"

"Exactly. And he to share in ours. That's a wonderful thing to remember when we're in trouble and need extra grace from God."

Even though she no longer had a leading role in the Propagation of the Faith (she was still an officer, but the most important posts were held by men), Pauline's interest in the work never wavered. By now she fully realized that she would never have been able to organize things on their present large and impressive scale. That task had been reserved for others. Thus, when certain of her friends among the Reparatrices complained that she was being unfairly treated, that Father Inglesi was acting as though he had originated everything and accepting compliments to which he had no right, she was able to see things in their true light.

"No, no, don't feel sorry for me," she urged. "This work is bigger than any one person. I did my part in the beginning, and now others are doing theirs."

Presently Father Inglesi went to Paris, taking with him a sizeable sum from the Propagation of the Faith which he promised to turn over to the proper authorities. But when a month had passed and there was still no word from him, the officers grew worried. Then came a letter from Bishop Dubourg of New Orleans, stating that Father Inglesi had never been authorized to collect for the American missions or for any other religious cause. He was an impostor through and through.

Naturally everyone was distressed. What a blow for their newly-organized society! Why, if word of what had happened should ever leak out, no one would have any faith in it. . . .

"We'll just have to keep the whole thing a secret," the officers decided. "It's the only wise and charitable thing to do."

But even as they made their decision, they remembered Pauline's original reluctance to have anything to do with Father Inglesi. Only twenty-two years old at the time of his arrival in Lyons, she had shown more good sense than any one of them.

CHAPTER 10

A NEW DIRECTION FOR PAULINE

In December, 1823, twenty-six-year-old Phileas Jaricot was ordained to the priesthood. Of all the family Pauline especially was proud and happy, for now her brother would be able to go to China to make converts to the Faith. But within just a few weeks her hopes were shattered. According to the superiors in Paris, Phileas was not strong enough for missionary life. He would have to content himself with working in France.

The young priest hid his disappointment as best he could. "I've decided to stay in Paris," he told Pauline presently. "Perhaps I can be of some use in visiting the prisons and hospitals."

"Of course you can," said Pauline encouragingly. "And if we pray hard and have faith, God may give you good health again. Then you can go to China after all." But even as she spoke, her heart was heavy. During the past four years, Phileas had been working very hard at the Seminary. Now, how tired he looked, how thin and worn!

"It'll be a miracle if he's ever well again," she realized sadly.

Soon there was another trial. Father Wurtz decided that Pauline's health was none too good either. Of course she was not as busy with the Propagation of the Faith as she had been. Since its reorganization into a worldwide society, others had taken over all the important positions. However, she did spend a lot of time in helping the poor and sick.

"Child, there's such a thing as being so busy with good works that one forgets to listen to the voice of God," he told her one day. "So that won't happen to you, I want you to drop all outside work for three years."

Pauline was amazed. Was she hearing correctly? Why, these days dozens of people in Lyons were looking to her for help and encouragement! How could she possibly stop seeing them —the widows, the orphans, the sick—*and for three whole years?*

"Father, I'm perfectly well, and these poor people do need me," she protested respectfully. "As for listening to God's voice, you know I've always tried to give as much time as I can to the spiritual life."

Father Wurtz was unimpressed. "Well, now you'll give it all your time," he declared. "As for the people you've been helping—Sophie and Laurette can look after them."

Since Father Wurtz was her spiritual director, Pauline's commonsense told her that his words came from God and that she ought to obey him as though he were Christ Himself. However, it was none too easy to do this when it meant retiring from the active life which she found so satisfying. Many times, when she tried to pray, her thoughts kept wandering to her beloved poor, and it was a real struggle to keep from going to them. After all, even though her older sisters were kind and understanding, they did not know her friends as she knew them. And because of the pressure of work in their own homes, they might very easily forget to visit someone in need.

Poor Pauline! These were difficult days, and frequently she found herself plunged into deep gloom. Somehow God seemed to have forgotten her, and she was tempted to believe that she was wasting her time in trying to serve Him. After all, what had He done for her these last few years? He had allowed her to put the Propagation of the Faith on a sound basis, then given its management into the hands of others. He had inspired her to devote herself to the poor and needy, only to curtail this work, too, through the voice of her spiritual guide. Once this same guide had been understanding, but sometimes now he was almost like a stranger. He did not seem to be listening when she told him her troubles. He made light of everything, and soon was talking about problems that bothered him. France, for instance. It was surely a lost country. Never had there been such a godless place. People cared only about making money. Pleasure, ease, worldly power— these were the things that interested them. Certainly one day God would severely punish such spiritual blindness.

"Maybe so, but why can't Father be interested in *me*?" Pauline asked herself, miserable and confused beyond words. "Why can't he help *me* to be happy?" But even as these thoughts crossed her mind, she dismissed them with a shudder. How dreadful to be wondering if the good and holy director whom God had sent her way was to be trusted! To be considering, even for a moment, that perhaps she ought to be looking for another!

"I'm a selfish, good-for-nothing wretch," she decided. "And there's just one thing to do about that. I'll offer myself as a victim for sinners. I'll ask God to let me suffer for the sins of France. He'll surely hear that prayer, and send me peace."

However, Father Wurtz was not in favor of such a plan. In fact, he was dismayed at what he considered to be dangerous presumption. "Child, you're acting as though you were a great saint," he said reprovingly. "Don't let me hear any more about such a thing. God wants you to live for Him, not to die."

Once again Pauline was plunged into gloom. Could it be true (as so many people were saying) that Father Wurtz was growing a little peculiar? Through the years he had made many enemies in Lyons by his forthright criticism of various matters concerning Church and State. Now even several of the clergy were opposed to his ideas, and had suggested that he be forbidden to preach.

"Dear Lord, what *am* I going to do?" thought Pauline anxiously.

In 1825, after she had been living quietly at home for two years, the long-expected blow fell. Despite the fact that he was sick and penniless, with no relatives at hand to whom he could turn for help, the authorities decided that sixty-year-old Father Wurtz ought to retire from public life. He was a good man and a holy priest, of course, but his writings were causing a lot of unfortunate gossip. It would be best for all concerned if he gave up parish work.

Pauline was distressed beyond words. What a way to treat a man who was in poor health and without any means of support! "Father, please come and live with us!" she urged. "I know Papa and I can make you comfortable. As for the ones responsible for all this trouble. . . ."

But Father Wurtz, although gratefully accepting the Jaricot

hospitality, would not listen to a word of reproach against his enemies. "No, no, child. All this is God's Will," he said quietly. "Let's bear it patiently and turn it to good account for heaven."

Pauline said no more, overcome with remorse that she had ever doubted any decisions of this good old priest. Certainly from now on she would strive to make up to him for this and other failings. Anthony, too, was extremely eager to help. Comfortable quarters for Father Wurtz must be prepared at once, he declared, and one of the servants detailed to see to his needs. Their guest was also to have a generous allowance to spend as he saw fit.

"Father will make his home with us for as long as he wishes," he told Pauline. "And don't let him worry about anything. He's doing us a real honor by coming here to live."

However, the need for such generosity lasted only a year. On October 1, 1826, an excited servant came running to Anthony Jaricot with the news that he had just found Father Wurtz dead in his room. Apparently he had slipped peacefully away, without the least struggle or pain.

Pauline was immeasurably shocked and saddened. Just ten years ago Father Wurtz had changed the course of her whole life. She had been not quite seventeen then—frivolous, vain, light-headed—attracted to the things of the world and yet aware that they could never bring her real happiness. Inspired by God, Father Wurtz had helped her to turn away from these and to say "yes" to what He wanted. Now that she was well past twenty-seven—

"Father, keep on helping me!" she begged. "Don't ever leave me alone. . . ."

The days following the death of her spiritual director were sad ones for Pauline. The big house seemed so empty, and there was the added trial that her own father's health was visibly failing. What was to be done? Of course it was only right that she stay with him a good part of the time. On the other hand, the three years of retirement which Father Wurtz had ordered were at an end. And even though the Society for the Propagation of the Faith was now in other hands, surely there was some new work which she might find to do?

It was just a few weeks later that Pauline felt her prayers were answered. A Jesuit priest, Father Joseph Barelle, wrote to ask if she could not procure for him some good books for children. He was a professor at the College of Billom, and very busy with his classes, but he had a hobby, too. This was to help a number of underprivileged young people to a better knowledge and love of the Catholic faith.

"The future of France is in the hands of youngsters like these," he wrote. "If we encourage them to read about God and His saints now, it may change the history of our country."

Remembering that Pope Leo the Twelfth had recently urged all loyal Catholics to promote the cause of good reading, Pauline consulted with some friends in Lyons who were active in the distribution of rosaries, crucifixes and other devotional objects. To her great joy, they promised to aid her in a project similar to that of Father Barelle, but on a larger scale and for varied age groups. However, as she set about collecting books and pamphlets, Pauline was struck by the thought that good reading in itself would never be enough to save France. Prayer was the thing—simple, honest, fervent, ceaseless—and not only from boys and girls but from persons of every age and class.

"An Association of Prayer is what we need," she told herself. "That, added to the good reading, could work wonders. Especially if the prayer had some thought behind it, like meditation on the mysteries of the Rosary...."

Suddenly she was aglow with eagerness. The Rosary was no longer popular in France because people did not realize its marvelous power for good. Certainly the daily recitation of fifteen mysteries, or even five, was something few among the laity would dream of undertaking. But surely *one* mystery a day—two minutes of thoughtful prayer—was not beyond the scope of anyone, even of children? And if a group of five such people could be formed, then another and another, the complete Rosary would come alive again. In a sense, God would be forced to pour out so much grace upon France that thousands would be converted....

"A Living Rosary!" Pauline thought, more excited than she had been in a long time. "I do believe it would work!"

CHAPTER 11

OBJECTIONS AGAINST THE ROSARY

The Reparatrices of the Heart of Jesus (Pauline's old friends among the women silk workers in Saint-Vallier and Lyons), all agreed that the new scheme was a wonderful one. And they were overjoyed to hear that now Pauline would be coming out of retirement. Several groups of five were formed immediately, each member pledged to the daily recitation of a different mystery of the Rosary. And it was decided that annual dues, ranging from fifteen cents to a dollar, would be collected by one of the five and the proceeds devoted to the distribution of Catholic books and pamphlets, as well as rosaries, statues, medals and other devotional objects.

Pauline saw with joy the success of her new work. This time she had remembered to secure the approval of the Archbishop, and within a few weeks the Association of the Living Rosary had been established in several local parishes. Everyone was enthusiastic, especially Father Barelle, who now had more than enough suitable books to distribute among his young friends. True, at first the Master General of the Dominican Order had been a bit disturbed to learn that in Lyons a young woman of twenty-seven was launching an organization to promote the Rosary on a large scale, and that varying sums of money were being given into her hands. After all, the Rosary had always been the special concern of Saint Dominic's family. And it was a prayer, not a scheme for making money.

"Who is this Pauline Jaricot?" he demanded. "And what's she up to?"

Pauline lost no time in setting things straight. The Association of the Living Rosary had two aims, she explained. First, to bring the people of France to a prayerful way of life by easy stages; second, to promote good reading habits. All funds collected were to be used for the purchase and distribution of Catholic books and pamphlets, plus various devotional articles for the home. God willing, these two works would help to make France a really Christian country again.

"I'm convinced that the mere distribution of alms and pious books will produce no fruit unless it is accompanied by prayer," she wrote the Dominican superior. "Among the treasures the Church has collected, the Rosary seems to us to respond best to our needs."

When the Master General read Pauline's letter, all his doubts vanished. Here was an honest young woman whose apostolic spirit resembled that of Saint Dominic himself. Without delay he sent her his blessing, and urged a continuation of the work. After all, how true it was that the Rosary was a treasure. Offered humbly, and in good faith, it had an enormous power against the forces of evil.

Pauline was immeasurably encouraged. For years she had had a devotion to Saint Dominic, and had always found inspiration in the famous motto of his Order: *Contemplare, et contemplata aliis tradere*—to contemplate, and to give to others the fruit of one's contemplation. And when she remembered that in the thirteenth century Saint Dominic and his followers

"WHO IS THIS PAULINE JARICOT?"

had overcome the Albigensian heresy largely through inspiring union among the faithful by a devotion to the Holy Rosary, fresh courage stirred within her. If the Rosary had saved France once, it could surely save it again. In fact, it *must* save it!

However, even though the Living Rosary was making friends on all sides, there were occasional difficulties in explaining its aims to certain people.

"I don't see any sense in saying the Hail Mary over and over again," one prospective woman member told Pauline. "It's just childish."

"That's right," put in another. "Besides, it makes a person's mind wander."

"Yes," agreed a third. "It'd be far better to speak to God in our own way, and when there's need for it, than to bother with the prayers of someone else when we're not in the mood for them."

Such objections were well known to Pauline. In fact, she had several good friends who had been brought up to find the Rosary so distasteful that they rarely offered it at all. The Blessed Virgin was the greatest of God's creatures, they admitted, the Queen of All Saints, but surely an endless repetition of Hail Marys in her honor was scarcely necessary for salvation? Of course such a practice could be very helpful for simple peasant folk. Likewise for children, and for the sick and aged who could not manage to do more. But certainly it was rather beneath any educated man or woman.

For a moment Pauline reflected upon such matters. Then suddenly she startled her companions by cheerfully admitting the force of their various arguments. Yes, saying the Hail Mary

over and over again was somewhat childish. Frequently it did
cause the mind to wander. And honest conversation with God,
in the privacy of one's soul, was on a far higher level than
ordinary vocal prayers. But then, what about faith?

Puzzled, the women looked at one another in doubtful silence. "Why, what do you mean?" asked one finally.

Pauline's eyes shone. "Don't you believe that the archangel
Gabriel spoke to Our Lady in words that pleased her? That
God inspired him to say 'Hail, full of grace, the Lord is with
thee'?"

"Well. . . ."

"Of course you do. And so does every other good Christian."

The women were not convinced. "But there's so much to
understand about the Rosary!" objected the first. "So many
things we don't know about the life of Our Lord and the
Blessed Virgin!"

Her two companions nodded in vigorous agreement. "Yes,"
said one. "And if we start worrying about such problems while
trying to say the Hail Marys, it only makes for confusion."

"That's right. Really, Pauline, offering the Rosary is nothing
but a chore. And a tiresome chore at that."

Pauline hesitated, recalling that another good friend, a wise
and holy Ursuline by the name of Mother Saint Lawrence, had
experienced these very same difficulties. And yet, when things
had been explained to her—

Suddenly she began to smile at the little group before her.
"Remember what I said about faith?" she asked cheerfully.

The second woman shrugged. "Yes, about God's inspiring

the archangel Gabriel to speak the right words to Our Lady. But I still don't understand. . . ."

"It's not necessary to understand," said Pauline quickly. "The main thing is to *do*. And I'm quite sure there's more merit in offering Our Lady a prayer that's difficult for us, as an act of faith, than in giving her one we find easy and attractive."

"But Pauline—"

"Or we could put it this way. Suppose you had been on earth when the Holy Family were living, and you knew they were partial to a certain kind of flower. Wouldn't you try your best to get it for them, even though you yourself preferred another?"

For a moment the women looked uneasily at one another. Pauline's sincerity and earnestness had succeeded in putting the problem in a new light. What a thought—that private devotion could have an element of selfishness about it! While as for that offered by members of the Living Rosary, that group prayer made up of words inspired by God Himself. . . .

"You *are* a clever girl, Pauline," said the first woman reluctantly. "I'm almost tempted to believe what you say."

The second hesitated, still a trifle ill at ease. "Yes. And we didn't mean to be disrespectful about the Rosary. If there's really room in your little group for people like us. . . ."

The third woman squared her shoulders. "Enough talk," she declared briskly. "We'll all join your Association, my dear —even though it hurts!"

With difficulty Pauline managed to hide her true feelings. What great gifts Our Lady of the Rosary must have in store for such friends as these! It was going to take an unusual amount of faith for them to persevere in offering even one mystery a day of her favorite prayer. But since faith was a virtue very dear to Our Lady's heart, one she always blessed in a special way. . . .

"Good," she said in a matter-of-fact voice. "I knew you'd understand."

Her words gave no hint of the joy she really felt. Three more members for the Association of the Living Rosary! Three more to pray that soon France would return to Christ! What if there were difficulties? Wasn't Our Lady the Mirror of Justice? Of course! She would reward even the smallest prayer offered in her honor, no matter how weak and imperfect.

CHAPTER 12

POISONING AT THE HOSPITAL

Phileas agreed. The Rosary could work wonders for those who said it, as well as for those for whom it was said.

"You mustn't let anything keep you from making it known and loved," he declared.

Once again Pauline felt her spirits rise. How good of God to let her have a share in such a wonderful work! Of course there were some people (as there had been in the early days of the Propagation of the Faith), who did not think a young woman ought to be taking an active part in Church affairs. It would be far better to leave such things to priests. But when the Papal Nuncio to France gave the new movement his unqualified blessing, most of the criticism died away.

Now it seemed as if there was only one thing for Pauline to worry about: the continued poor health of her brother Phileas. For despite the best of medical care and the many prayers offered for him since Ordination by family and friends, he had never recovered his strength. Finally he had come to agree with the superiors in Paris that he was not meant to be a Chinese missionary, and in 1827, when he had been a priest for four years, he accepted the position of head chaplain at the Hotel-Dieu, one of the largest hospitals in Lyons.

74

However, instead of having a happy and satisfying life here, thirty-year-old Phileas soon found himself surrounded with all manner of unpleasantness. He was too much the reformer, said certain disgruntled members of the staff. He had made a number of rules that irked everyone and had even dismissed several long-time employees. If there was to be any peace at the hospital, he would have to be dismissed himself and another chaplain found.

"Nonsense!" exclaimed Sophie Perrin when she heard the news. "It's high time the Hotel-Dieu had a man like Phileas in charge. Why, the place is filthy, the nurses ignorant, and half the patients die from lack of care!"

Laurette and Victor Chartron agreed. Once the Hotel-Dieu had been a splendid institution with a group of self-sacrificing nuns in charge. But the Revolution of 1789 had changed all that. Those Sisters who would not swear allegiance to the godless new government had been replaced by irreligious and inexperienced lay people. These in turn had appointed their own officials, so that now the hospital was governed by a number of selfish individuals who did not have the patients' interests at heart. They were more concerned with the money their positions brought them than in helping the sick to recover.

From her experience in visiting other hospitals in Lyons, Pauline well knew the problems facing Phileas. For instance, he had replaced certain undesirable nurses with a few women who had a genuine love for the sick. These, under his guidance, were leading a semi-religious life and some day hoped to become a real community—the Sisters of Bon Secours. In the meantime, he had rented a small house for them out of his own income, to which they could retire for rest and prayer.

Then, too, he was doing his best to stop certain abuses, such as petty thievery from the patients and waste of food and linen. But how his enemies fought him at every turn! Some had even gone so far as to threaten bodily harm to the zealous young chaplain if he continued his reforms.

"Poor Phileas! We must pray hard for him," Pauline told herself uneasily. "He's really leading a martyr's life at the hospital."

Two years later, on October 11, 1829, there was even more cause for anxiety. Thirty-seven-year-old Laurette Chartron, ailing for several months, took a sudden turn for the worse and died. And her heartbroken husband, left alone with their five young children, could not bring himself to accept the trial in the right spirit.

"Don't talk to me of God and His mercy!" he burst out when Pauline tried to comfort him. "You've been wrapped up in religion so long that you've forgotten what it is to be human."

"But Victor—"

"No, no! I don't want to hear a word. Laurette was the best wife in all the world. It's not fair that she had to die so young."

Pauline's heart was heavy. Her brother-in-law was a good man, and had been a wonderful help in those early days when she had been trying to organize the Propagation of the Faith. In fact, it was at his factory in Saint-Vallier that she had found the first of her Reparatrices. Then, more recently, Victor had also taken an active part in the Association of the Living Rosary. But now when he himself was so much in need of help—

"Don't worry, dear," said Sophie kindly. "Everything's going to be all right. And try not to be hurt by Victor's attitude. He's not himself these days, and doesn't realize what he's saying."

However, even Sophie found it hard to bear the blow which presently followed when certain lay helpers at the Hotel-Dieu, angered by the reforms which Phileas continued to make, decided to frighten away the thirty-two-year-old chaplain by placing poison in his food.

"We've had enough of this upstart priest," they told one another. "Maybe now he'll get out and leave us in peace."

But Phileas, although shocked and hurt and in great pain after the poisoning, was not to be intimidated. When he finally recovered and had enjoyed a short rest at Nice, he announced that he was returning to his work at the Hotel-Dieu.

"I won't give in to these people," he told his sisters grimly. "The sick need me, and the good nurses I'm trying to train in the religious life."

Pauline and Sophie looked at each other in dismay. Surely this was not wise. Phileas' enemies were cruel and ruthless men. They would stop at nothing to get rid of him.

In just a few months these fears were justified. Early in the spring of 1830 there was a second attempt to poison Phileas, and this time he did not rally.

"Look after my nursing Sisters!" he gasped, as Pauline, summoned hastily from her work at home, gazed in horror at her brother's agonized face. Then, a few hours later: "The Will of God be done. I have tried to work for Him. . . ."

CHAPTER 13

SAINT PHILOMENA

Phileas' death at the early age of thirty-three was a heavy cross for Pauline, Sophie and Paul, especially as they were haunted by thoughts of the evil that had brought it about. Then, too, how closely their brother's passing had followed upon that of Laurette!

"Papa will be next," they told one another sorrowfully. "He's not been himself for a long time."

Anthony Jaricot had grown increasingly feeble, and in recent months his mind had been affected, so that now he was often childish. His devoted servant Henry seldom left his side, and this relieved Pauline of much responsibility, but it did not lessen her grief at the impending loss of her father. However, she tried to forget her troubles in work, especially in the enormous correspondence connected with the Living Rosary. For in the three years of its existence the Association had grown by leaps and bounds, spreading into many parts of Europe, Canada, the United States, South America, India, Smyrna and Turkey. Each month Pauline wrote a circular letter to all the members, urging them to continue the good work. And she wrote to interested priests and Bishops, too, explaining the aims of the Association.

There was also another work which took considerable time: the care of Phileas' group of nurses from the Hotel-Dieu. After his death they had gone to live at Nazareth, the little house he had rented for them as a rest home. Now Sophie purchased it outright. And since Pauline had promised her brother on his deathbed that she would look after these charges of his, she went to visit them frequently, no matter how busy she was, and saw that they wanted for nothing.

Nazareth was in a charming spot, close to the hilltop chapel of Our Lady of Fourvière, one of the most famous shrines in Lyons. However, there was another and much larger house nearby, with spacious lawns and gardens and a magnificent view of the city, and presently Pauline began to ponder the wisdom of acquiring this property, too. It would make an ideal headquarters for the Association of the Living Rosary, with plenty of space to store the membership records and vast correspondence, as well as the ever-growing collection of books, pamphlets and religious articles destined for distribution among the needy. Yet for some months she hesitated about taking such a step, half-convinced that it was God's Will for her to leave the world and become a Visitation nun. Of course entrance into the cloister would mean giving the work of the Living Rosary into the hands of others. But what of that? It would surely continue to prosper, even as the Society for the Propagation of the Faith had done since she had withdrawn from active participation ten years ago.

But when she discussed matters with Father Renault, her Jesuit director, he urged her to remain where she was. God had given her definite talents for organization and for making friends, he said. It would be best if she put these to use among lay people like herself.

"The Living Rosary is a wonderful work, Pauline," he pointed out. "I think you'd better devote your life to it."

So, after more thought and prayer, Pauline bought the large

house near Our Lady's chapel and named it Loreto. However, it was much in need of repair, and so it was some time before she could move into it. But finally in August, 1832, came the longed-for day when she and several of Phileas' nurses went there to live.

Naturally the move aroused much comment in Lyons. What was thirty-three-year-old Pauline up to now? Why wasn't she staying at home with her poor old father instead of buying an expensive country estate and going there to live with a number of pious women?

"Maybe she's starting a religious community," someone suggested.

Pauline's heart beat fast when she heard the rumor. Often she had cherished that very hope. She had even chosen a name for her little family—the Daughters of Mary. Their special aim would be to lead a hidden and prayerful life in reparation for the sins of France. They would have great devotion to the Rosary, and to the Way of the Cross. And of course they would pray very hard for social reforms that would give a just wage and decent living conditions to every working man in France and so pave the way for the return of this whole group to the Church.

However, the women who had come to Loreto were not much interested in this idea. They wanted to be nursing Sisters as Phileas had planned, rather than cloistered religious. Pauline was wise enough not to argue the point. In their case, she realized, God would be best served by active works of mercy, and so presently the little house of Nazareth was made into a hospital for incurables and given into their care.

By the spring of 1834 the activities at Nazareth and Loreto

were well-known to everyone in Lyons. Scarcely a day passed that pilgrims from Our Lady's chapel at Fourvière did not drop in for a visit. Loreto, in particular, was besieged by visitors, for as headquarters for the Association of the Living Rosary it had become known to thousands of people. Then, too, missionaries back in Europe after years of labor abroad often made it a point to stop and thank Pauline for her part in organizing the Society for the Propagation of the Faith. What untold good she had accomplished by interesting people in the foreign missions! The pennies she had collected had meant food, clothing, churches and schools for the poorest of the poor, as well as the priceless gift of Faith.

"God bless you for everything," they said gratefully.

Deeply touched by the sincerity of these priests, Pauline always tried to explain that for years she had had no official connection with the Propagation of the Faith. Abler hands than hers had long since taken over details, and it was due to the efforts of these new workers that the Society had grown in strength and numbers and now was able to do so much. But the missionaries only listened politely, smiled and shook their heads.

"My dear, you're too modest," said one of them one day. "You founded the Society for the Propagation of the Faith. The others have merely followed where you led."

Presently a priest came to Loreto whom Pauline knew well. He was Father de Magallon of the Brothers of Saint John of God. Owing to various political troubles in Italy, his community had come to France some years ago, and from the beginning the Jaricot family had helped him generously with alms. Now, in order to show his appreciation, he had brought

Pauline a most unusual gift. In fact, it was beyond price, being a major relic of Saint Philomena and the only one of its kind in France.

Naturally Pauline was delighted, and lost no time in showing her treasure to Marie Melquiond, one of Phileas' nurses who had decided to live at Loreto in order to help with the work of the Living Rosary.

"Aren't we lucky, Marie?" she burst out. "Here's one of the bones of that little martyr Father Vianney was telling us about on his last visit. He prays to her every day, and she does the most wonderful things for him. Remember?"

Marie's eyes shone. Who could forget how the forty-eight-year-old pastor of Ars had praised Saint Philomena on his last visit to Loreto? It was she, he had insisted, who was responsible for all the marvelous cures and conversions which were bringing thousands of people to Ars and making his parish church the most famous pilgrimage spot in all France.

"I certainly do remember!" she exclaimed, kissing the relic fervently. "Welcome to Loreto, little saint! And work some miracles for us, too!"

Soon everyone at Nazareth and Loreto was clamoring for more details about Philomena. Who was she, anyway? When had she lived? How had she died? When was her feast day?

Recalling what Father de Magallon had told her, Pauline did her best to piece together Philomena's story. But it was a difficult task, since actually very little was known. Indeed, until 1802 no one had even heard of Philomena. Then, while making new excavations in the catacombs beneath Rome, some workmen had come upon a grave with three stone slabs bearing a Latin inscription: *Pax tecum Filumena,* or *Peace be with*

"AREN'T WE LUCKY, MARIE?"

you, beloved. There were also crude drawings of three arrows,
two anchors and an olive branch upon the stones.

"When the slabs were pried loose, the workmen found the
skeleton of a young girl, perhaps thirteen or fourteen years
of age," Pauline explained. "Apparently 'Filumena' or ' Beloved' had lived in the first or second century, and possibly
she had been shot to death by arrows for the Faith."

There was a flurry of excitement among the listeners. "She
started working miracles right away, Pauline?"

"No, not for three years or so. Her bones were taken to
Naples, and the Bishop there put them inside a little statue.
He asked a woman suffering from cancer to dress the statue.
No sooner had she begun the task than she felt herself cured."

"How wonderful!"

"Yes, but that's not all. The night before the relics were
to be taken to their final resting place in the nearby town of
Mugnano, a lawyer was cured of sciatica when he touched
them, and a noble lady of a painful ulcer on her hand."

"The relics are still at Mugnano?"

"Yes. And what wonders Philomena has done in that little
town! Why, the place is famous because of her!"

However, Pauline had to admit that as yet—some thirty
years later—Philomena had never been canonized, and the
term "Saint" was applied to her only because of the great
popular devotion that had grown up in Italy. But some day
the Holy Father, Pope Gregory the Sixteenth, would surely
raise this child to the altar. After all, she had worked miracles.
And she had given her life for the Faith. . . .

"Let's pray for Philomena's canonization," she suggested.
"If we do, I'm sure she'll bless our work in all kinds of ways."

CHAPTER 14

UPRISING!

Soon everyone at Nazareth and Loreto had developed a great devotion to Philomena. Pauline herself prayed fervently to the little martyr for the intentions closest to her heart: the success of the foreign missions and the Living Rosary, the well-being of her friends and family, above all that something would soon be done to improve conditions for the working class in France. Since 1830 there had been a growing unrest among the workers, with numerous strikes and violence. The factory owners viewed these uprisings only with alarm, but Pauline's heart was with the workers. Why shouldn't they have higher wages, shorter working hours and decent homes in which to raise their children? This was only reasonable and fair. Yet so many wealthy people in Lyons were afraid to give in to any of these legitimate demands.

"That's not the Christian way," she told herself indignantly. "If only I could do something to help...."

Her friends did not like to see Pauline worrying so much about the workers. Lately she herself had not been at all well, a troublesome growth on one lung not having responded to treatment. And her heart was bothering her, too.

"Why not pray to little Philomena for a cure?" they urged. "That's more important than anything."

"I *am* praying," Pauline admitted, "and much harder than you think."

But one day early in April of that same year, 1834, Pauline's condition became so grave that a priest was called and the Last Sacraments administered. Everyone at Nazareth and Loreto prepared to hear at any hour of her death. The next day, however, she was still holding her own against her illness, but on that very day the social tension which had been mounting steadily for months broke its bonds. Once again the workers rose against the factory owners, and soon government troops were pouring into Lyons with orders to put down the revolt at all costs. Shots were fired and bullets whizzed in the streets, shattering glass and starting fires where they reached their targets, or, more often, missed them. All who could fled the city; those who were unable to escape barricaded themselves in the cellars of their homes. Desperate mobs surged in every part of the city, and the black flag of the rebels was raised over one captured building after another.

"Poor, poor people!" murmured Pauline from her sickbed. "What's going to become of them?"

Marie Melquiond had trouble in restraining her tears. Pauline was so ill, scarcely able to breathe, and still she was concerned about the workers—even praying for them!

"Do try to rest," she pleaded. "Everything will soon be under control."

But who could rest with the city in a state of siege? With the explosion of shots, the rumbling of cannon, the shouts of the mob, the screaming of the wounded? There was also the danger of a great fire, for early in the revolt the workers had set several bridges ablaze in an effort to halt the arrival of fresh government troops, and in the turmoil how easily one of the smaller conflagrations could get out of control!

That night smoke was still rising from the city and the sky overhead was reddened with flame. Several terrified women came up from Lyons to beg for shelter at Loreto. Pauline's house was on Fourvière, a hill dedicated to Our Lady, and it had a chapel, too. Surely it was a safe place to stay?

Hesitantly Marie Melquiond led the visitors inside. "It's not much safer here than anywhere else," she said. "But of course you're welcome. And we do have food."

However, after a sleepless night spent in the cold and darkened chapel (Pauline lying on a mattress on the floor), the group realized they were in grave danger. The dawn had brought hostilities even closer to Loreto, and presently a bullet struck a window, another tore through the wall across their heads, while the force of new explosions jarred the altar and jolted loose several of the pews.

"Maybe we ought to try to reach the cave," suggested Pauline's butcher, who had also taken refuge at Loreto. "If we stay here much longer, we'll all be killed."

Pauline nodded weakly. The cave at the far end of the garden would make an ideal shelter. Years ago, during the great Revolution, it had served as a hiding place for priests. And since very few people knew about it. . . .

"I think you're right," she admitted. "Let's go right away."

But the gardener, who had also spent the night at Loreto, was doubtful about such a plan. There was a side door opening into the yard which could be reached without difficulty. But what would they do once they were outside? The cave was at a considerable distance. And since food and water must be taken along, and the mistress of the house was far too ill to walk—

Pauline mustered a smile as she struggled for breath. "Don't worry," she whispered. "We'll be all right. Our Lord will go with us."

Marie Melquiond stared. "You mean the Blessed Sacrament, Pauline?"

"Yes. The Tabernacle is portable. I can hold it in my arms."

Soon the little procession was on its way, the two men carrying Pauline on her mattress, the women following close behind with food and other supplies. Bullets whizzed dangerously near as they hurried down the long garden path, but no one was hit and finally they reached the cave. This was a fairly spacious structure, with sides that branched out in the form of a cross. Pauline's mattress was set down in the widest part, the Tabernacle beside her, and then all fell to their knees in thanksgiving. They were safe, at least for the present.

"We shouldn't be here . . . too long!" Pauline managed to gasp after a moment. "A day or two, at the most. . . ."

But no one was deceived. The fighting might go on for a week or more. Also, it was greatly to be feared that before long the rebels would discover their hiding place. However, at nightfall they were still safe. Around noon the following day they decided it would not be amiss to receive Holy Communion. After all, the circumstances were unusual. And they had been fasting since midnight.

"Dear Lord, please look after Papa!" begged Pauline, as she lay back upon her mattress to make her thanksgiving. "Keep him safe at home with the servants. And keep us safe, too . . . if it be Your holy Will. . . ."

CHAPTER 15

TRIP TO ROME

For several days the group remained in hiding. Occasionally the butcher and the gardener slipped outside, despite the danger from stray bullets, to see what was going on. But when they returned, pale-faced and shaken, it was always with the same news. The black flags of the rebels were still flying from the public buildings in Lyons, and shells were bursting everywhere.

"It's a good thing we didn't stay at the house," they told the women grimly. "It's been hit dozens of times."

Pauline tried to be cheerful, urging her friends to recite the Rosary and other prayers to Our Lady. She called for help from Saint Philomena, too, since she probably had endured fear like theirs in the days of persecution in Rome. But despite her bravest efforts, it was very hard not to give in to discouragement, especially when pain stabbed her chest. Indeed, as she lay helpless upon her mattress hour after hour, Pauline often felt that for herself it was really useless to be calling on heaven for help. Her time on earth was about over.

"Lord, accept me as a victim!" she prayed. "I give myself to You in the cause of peace—and for the poor, misguided workers of France. . . ."

However, on the morning of the fourth day the roar of

89

cannon was not to be heard, whereupon there was considerable speculation among the occupants of the cave as to what this might mean.

"Perhaps there's been a miracle of sorts and those wretched rebels have run out of ammunition," suggested the butcher hopefully.

"Perhaps," said the gardener. "Let's go and see."

In just a little while the men were back, their faces jubilant. The butcher had been right. The rebels were out of ammunition, and all over the city the black flags were being hauled down as government troops took control. Now it was safe to return to the house—even to go up the hill to Our Lady's shrine at Fourvière where a Mass of Thanksgiving was about to be celebrated.

"Thank God!" cried Pauline when she heard the news, and she urged her friends to go at once to hear Mass. She would be all right by herself, she assured them, until they returned. They were also to tell the chaplain at Fourvière that she would like to receive Holy Communion. And of course the Tabernacle ought to be taken back to the chapel at Loreto. God willing, not too much damage had been done there, and the Blessed Sacrament might be restored to the altar.

Although peace had now been reestablished in Lyons, it was several weeks before conditions were in any sense normal. The workers still bore their grievances. Only physically had the rebellion been put down. Pauline wept when she heard that five hundred people had been killed in the uprising. To think that nothing had been accomplished by all the pain and suffering of those dreadful April days! Still there were the low wages, long hours and miserable living conditions for the workers. Their employers had learned nothing.

"If there was just something I could *do!*" she thought wearily, acknowledging that the Jaricot fortune had been built upon the labors of this same underprivileged class. But what could she do? Her heart was in such a weakened condition that for days at a time she could not leave her bed. On her better days she was able to sit in a chair for an hour or so and write a few letters. Then she found herself utterly exhausted. And on December 26, when her eighty-year-old father passed away, she felt that she herself would soon follow.

However, in the spring of 1835, Pauline was gripped by an unusual conviction. She was an invalid, yes, but Saint Philomena would cure her if she would only make a pilgrimage to Mugnano, near Naples, and pray at her tomb!

Naturally everyone was aghast when she announced her intention. A six-hundred-mile trip by lumbering stagecoach to Italy? Through the hazardous passes of the Alps? Impossible!

"My dear, you couldn't breathe in that high mountain air," protested Marie Melquiond. "Even people in good health, with strong hearts, find it difficult."

Pauline nodded. "I know. But Philomena will see to everything. We'll be all right."

"*We?*"

"Yes. Oh, Marie, I want you to come along, too! I'm sure the Holy Father will grant new blessings to the members of the Living Rosary if we talk to him in person. And you know this trip to Mugnano makes a fine excuse for stopping over in Rome...."

Marie Melquiond scarcely knew what to say. Pauline seemed to have forgotten that her heart was about ready to give out; that she had not been able to leave the house in months, and that even when she did spend an hour or two in the garden, she had to be carried there in a chair.

"My dear, you couldn't possibly go to Mugnano, or to Rome either," she said regretfully. "It wouldn't be prudent."

Pauline was playfully indignant. "Father de Magallon doesn't think so. He says Saint Philomena will cure me if I just have faith."

But Marie was not to be swayed. The superior of the Brothers of Saint John of God (who had given Pauline her relic of the little martyr) was a holy man, of course, but certainly not a doctor.

"No," she said firmly. "You'd better forget about the whole thing, Pauline. And especially my part in it."

However, Pauline could not bring herself to forget, and early that same summer she succeeded in persuading both Marie Melquiond and Father Henry Rousselon, the chaplain at Loreto, to accompany her to Italy. Naturally they thought that she was going to her death, and they became certain of this when she fell seriously ill at Chambéry and had to be taken to the Visitation convent to rest. But presently she astonished everyone by saying that she felt better and insisting that the trip be resumed.

In the following days which saw their progress through the Alps and down into Italy, Marie seldom took her eyes off the invalid. How tired she looked, leaning against her pillows, how thin and worn! But her smile was still confident and she never complained, even when the carriage jolted her most painfully as it rolled southward over the hot, dusty roads.

"We don't have to visit Mugnano to see a miracle," Marie whispered to Father Rousselon one day. "We have one with us right now."

HOW TIRED SHE LOOKED!

The priest smiled grimly. "The trip's not over yet, though. Be prepared for the worst."

But the worst did not come, and around July 1 the little group arrived in Rome. However, by now Pauline was in a state of actual collapse, and poor Marie Melquiond was at her wits' end.

"We'd better ask the Religious of the Sacred Heart for hospitality," she decided. "Later on we'll see what can be done about an interview with the Holy Father."

Pauline smiled weakly. "Yes," she murmured. "Later on . . . in a day or two. . . ."

But although the Religious of the Sacred Heart gave their guest every attention, it was soon evident that a trip to the Vatican was impossible. Pauline had made the entire journey from France in an invalid's chair, but now she was no longer able to sit up at all.

"Bed's the only place for the poor girl," said Mother Madeleine Sophie Barat, the superior at the convent. "I think, when His Holiness hears that, he'll come to see her himself."

For the first time in many days Marie Melquiond felt her spirits rise. So the long, painful journey was not to be without fruit! "You really mean it, Mother?" she asked.

"Of course, my dear. After all, look at what your friend has done for the Church. Why, the Propagation of the Faith is known everywhere. And the Living Rosary, too."

"But—"

"There, now, don't worry. I'm sure everything will turn out all right. That is—"

"If Pauline lives?"

"Yes. If Pauline lives."

CHAPTER 16

THE TOWNSFOLK DEMAND A MIRACLE

$\mathcal{M}any$ prayers were offered for Pauline's recovery, but with no immediate result. Indeed, on the great day when Pope Gregory the Sixteenth came to the convent to give her his blessing and to thank her for all that she had done for the Church, she was still unable to leave her bed. However, such happiness filled her heart that for the time being she completely forgot that she was ill. What an honor to be visited by the Vicar of Christ on earth! To be urged by him to ask for favors, to explain what she had in mind for the Association of the Living Rosary! Almost at once her thin face took on fresh color as she roused herself to obey.

With His Holiness' permission, she suggested, perhaps the Association could eventually have its central office in Rome? There was also the matter of certain indulgences being granted to the members. Then, what about Philomena? Couldn't a study of her cause be made so that she would soon be canonized? After all, she was a martyr, and for more than thirty years had been working wonders of every description. . . .

Pope Gregory, together with Cardinal Lambruschini who had accompanied him, listened with grave attention to all that Pauline had to say and readily agreed with her suggestions about the Living Rosary. But it was clear to Mother Barat, who stood watching, that he was far less interested in Philomena's cause than in Pauline herself. What wonders she had done by her two great foundations—the Society for the Propagation of the Faith and the Association of the Living Rosary! And to think that she had organized both of these when she was only in her twenties!

"The good Lord must have a great reward in store for you, child," he said kindly.

Mother Barat had a sudden urge to tell what she had heard from Marie Melquiond about Pauline's other good works: the generous alms to one religious community after another; her motherly interest in the working class; the big house at Loreto where even now some twenty girls and women were being given their food, clothes and lodging. But she put the thought aside. It would be unwise to tire the invalid by prolonging the interview.

Apparently Pope Gregory had the same idea, for after a few minutes he prepared to take his leave. Bending over Pauline, he blessed her and begged that she remember him when she went to heaven.

"My daughter, that's a favor I really want," he said earnestly. "You'll not forget?"

Pauline's eyes shone with happiness as she looked up into the Pope's kindly face. "Oh, no, Your Holiness! I'll not forget. But on the other hand—"

"Yes, child?"

"What about Philomena? If she cures me at Mugnano, and I come to see you at the Vatican, walking like anyone else, you'll do something about her cause?"

The Pope smiled. "Of course. That would be a miracle of the first class." Then, turning to Cardinal Lambruschini: "I recommend my very dear daughter to you. Grant her all there is to be granted in the way of privileges and indulgences." Then to Mother Barat, in Italian: "Poor little thing, how ill she is! She'll never come back from Mugnano alive. . . ."

Pauline did not understand Italian, but she caught the meaning of the Pope's words. Yet far from being depressed after his departure, she was in excellent spirits.

"We'll be leaving soon for Mugnano," she told Marie Melquiond confidently. "That trip's not much more than a hundred miles. It won't be too hard."

However, it was all of five weeks before Pauline was able to leave the Religious of the Sacred Heart. In fact, her thirty-sixth birthday, July 22, was not the festive occasion it might have been because of the general concern about her health. But around the first of August she insisted that she was well enough to be off for Mugnano. What did it matter that the summer heat was at its worst? They would travel by night and so avoid most of the discomfort.

"Yes," agreed Marie doubtfully. "I suppose we could do that."

But Father Rousselon was as fearful as ever. "It's most unwise to start traveling again," he declared. "Pauline will die on the way this time. I'm sure of it."

Nevertheless they set out on schedule and on Saturday afternoon, August 8, arrived at Mugnano to find the town in a state of great excitement. The anniversary of the arrival there of Saint Philomena's relics was to be observed on Monday, and the streets and houses were gaily decked with garlands.

Colorful banners fluttered from the public buildings, while
the parish church—blazing with candles—was already crowded
with pilgrims from far and near.

Exhausted though she was, Pauline had herself taken to
Philomena's shrine at the first possible moment. Sympathetic
bystanders at once made a place for her wheelchair and smil-
ingly urged her to be of good heart. Philomena—*their* saint—
would cure her as she had cured so many other sick people.
Weren't her blessed bones only a few feet away, enshrined in
a magnificent tomb before the altar?

Pauline smiled her acknowledgment, then closed her eyes.
At last the long trip was over! She had accomplished what she
had set out to do, even more. In a few minutes, the choir
would be singing Vespers. How good of the little virgin
martyr to have arranged that three French pilgrims should
be in time for this beautiful service!

But Marie Melquiond was ill at ease. The church was un-
bearably hot and crowded, and Pauline looked as if she were
dead. Even the next morning, after a fair night's rest at a
neighboring inn, her breath was coming in thick, uneven gasps.
And though it might be Sunday, surely it was the height of
folly to take her to church again? However, Pauline would not
hear of remaining in her room. Nothing would do but that
she assist at Mass, receive Holy Communion at Philomena's
shrine, then venerate her relics, not once but several times in
the course of the day. And that she try to kneel before them,
too.

By now the case of the newly-arrived French lady had
aroused wide sympathy among the people of Mugnano, especially since they had discovered that she had come all the

way from Lyons to seek a cure through the intercession of their saint. Determined that such great faith must not go unrewarded, they began to watch for her various appearances and joined their petitions to hers as she prayed before the altar. But when a whole day had passed and their beloved wonderworker had failed to show forth her heavenly powers, the more excitable of the townsfolk began to grow impatient.

"Philomena, you've *got* to hear us!" cried one woman indignantly. "Don't you see this poor French lady's in great pain?"

"What's wrong?" demanded another. "Are you deaf, Philomena?"

"Why don't you do something?"

"Yes, look at all we've done for you!"

"Flowers for your statue!"

"And candles!"

"And alms for the poor!"

"And banners in the streets!"

"Hurry up, now! A miracle for the French lady!"

"Yes, a big miracle!"

"It's your duty, Philomena! You owe it to us!"

Pauline winced. Of course everyone meant well, but it was very embarrassing to be the cause of such a hubbub, especially in church.

"Please tell these good people to pray more quietly," she begged Marie. "It . . . it doesn't seem right to be making so much noise."

But all Marie's efforts were in vain. By now the people of Mugnano were convinced that the reputation of their beloved patroness was at stake, and presently several of them had in-

vaded the sanctuary and were pounding excitedly upon Philomena's tomb.

"Are you there, little saint?"

"What's the matter with you?"

"Why don't you answer?"

"Cure this poor French lady, or it's all over between us!"

Marie shrugged. One might as well tell the wind to stop
blowing, or the rain to cease falling, as to argue with these
indignant clients of Philomena.

CHAPTER 17

PHILOMENA'S RESPONSE

The next day, August 10, Pauline was taken to church several times. Despite the pilgrims' continued assurance that all was going to be well, she took up her accustomed place more dead than alive. Then, during the Benediction service which followed upon Vespers, tears began rolling down her cheeks. Marie, who was watching, leaned forward anxiously.

"What is it, dear? What's wrong?"

Pauline looked at her. "I . . . I think I'm going to die," she murmured. But there was no fear in her voice. Only relief and a childlike joy.

Marie looked around nervously. But before she could get anyone's attention to ask for assistance in raising the kneeling invalid to her wheelchair, Pauline's face took on fresh color. Her hands especially, hitherto so pale and limp, suddenly seemed warmer and more alive. Surely it couldn't be possible—

Pauline, reading her thoughts, motioned to her to put her head close. "I made a dreadful mistake, Marie," she whispered into her friend's ear. "I'm *not* dying, I'm getting well! The little saint is curing me! Somehow I think she really began to do it yesterday, but now . . . oh, how much better I feel!"

Marie stared in amazement. What was this? But at a pleading glance from Pauline, she knelt obediently and remained silent until long after the Benediction service was over. However when the church was practically empty of worshippers and the few who remained were absorbed in their prayers, she could control her excitement no longer, especially when she saw Pauline rise easily to her feet and step out into the aisle.

"Pauline! You're standing! And with no support!"

"Sssh, dear, I know. Look, now I'm going to try to walk to the door. . . ."

Utterly fascinated yet still unable to believe her eyes, Marie followed down the aisle, pushing the wheelchair before her. But it was not needed, for at the church door Pauline announced that she was going to walk back to the inn.

"Philomena *has* worked a miracle!" she exclaimed, joy and wonder shining in her eyes. "Oh, Marie, you know I haven't been up like this for fifteen months. . . ."

By now Marie was almost in tears. All this was too good to be true! But in a few minutes, after they had made their way down the street, then up a steep flight of stairs to their room at the inn, she realized that this was no delusion. Pauline was breathing normally. She was not in the least pale or tired. There *had* been a miracle through the intercession of little Philomena. . . .

"God be praised!" she burst out, then began to cry as though her heart would break.

However, there was little time for tears. Very soon there was a babble of voices down in the street. Then came a vigorous pounding at the door as the landlord demanded to know if it was really true that the French lady had walked all the way home from church. Certain people insisted they had seen

the wonder with their own eyes, and had told Father Francis
di Lucia, the parish priest. Now he was downstairs, and desperately eager to learn the truth.

"Yes, yes, it's true!" exclaimed Pauline, throwing wide the
door. "Philomena did cure me, just as you and everyone else
said she would!"

Within a few minutes the good news was all over Mugnano.
Church bells rang out triumphantly, and a huge crowd began
gathering under Pauline's window. What a wonderful, wonderful day! Once again the town's little patroness had proved
her heavenly powers.

"Long live Philomena!"

"Long live the French lady!"

"The *holy* French lady, you mean!"

"Yes, yes! Where is she now?"

"Bring her out!"

"Yes, we want the holy French lady!"

A bit hesitantly, Pauline went to the window to wave at
the assembled throng. But when a chorus of deafening cheers
rose up, as though she were some royal personage, she with-
drew in dismay. However, the parish priest, as flushed and
excited as his people, promptly led her back to the window.

"No, no, my dear, don't be shy! Can't you see all this is
for our little saint's glory?"

"But Father—"

"There, now, you owe it to Philomena to show what she's
done for you."

So Pauline remained at her window, bowing and waving,
while the church bells pealed forth and the whole town went
wild with joy.

It was a totally new experience, of course, and that night
Pauline fell into bed in a state of happy confusion. But the
next day, when Father Francis informed her that she was to
make a circuit of the town, accompanied by a military escort
and a brass band, she was appalled.

"Oh, no, Father, I couldn't!" she protested. "It wouldn't
be right. I'm not that important...."

"Nonsense, child, you're the most important person in
town!" declared the priest. "It's your duty to be seen, and
to tell everyone about the miracle. Come along, we're waiting
for you."

Pauline looked doubtfully at Marie Melquiond. Certainly
it would never do to be selfish and disappoint the good people
of Mugnano. But to parade about the town behind a brass
band—

Marie burst into uncontrollable laughter. "Oh, Pauline!"
she gasped when she recovered her voice. "You ... you look
so worried! But do go ahead. It must be the local custom.
And Father Francis is right, of course. You owe it to all those
who prayed for you."

So presently, under a hot August sun, Pauline found herself
on a triumphal march about the town, flanked by Mugnano's
leading citizens. Up one gaily decorated street and down the
next went the joyful procession, with trumpets blowing and
banners waving. Men left their work, women wept, dogs
barked, children threw flowers, and the air echoed to lusty
cheers from the hundreds crowding the line of march, as well
as to the booming of church bells.

"There's the holy French lady!"

"The one Philomena cured!"

"YOU'VE BEEN CURED, HAVEN'T YOU?"

105

"How pretty she is!"

"And how well she marches!"

"God be praised for the miracle!"

"Long live our little Philomena!"

"Long live the holy French lady!"

For several minutes, smiling and waving, Pauline stepped along dutifully with her companions to the gay music of the band. But presently she turned hopefully to Father Francis, who was marching beside her. "Father, isn't this enough?" she asked. "Couldn't we stop now?"

The priest stared in amazement. "Stop, my dear? *Now?* Of course not. Why, that would be an insult to our little saint!" Then, as Pauline gave a sigh: "Surely you're not getting tired?"

"A . . . a little, Father."

"Nonsense! You've been cured, haven't you? Come along, child. Step lively. Why, this is only the beginning!"

CHAPTER 18

ROME AGAIN

Father Francis knew whereof he spoke. The parade was only one of many public ceremonies to honor Pauline's cure. In fact, during the nine days she remained in Mugnano, there were numerous other tests which she was required to undergo to prove that her newly-restored health was not a myth. Most of these ordeals were devised by the parish priest himself, and Pauline frequently felt that they were far too rigorous. She could not possibly walk so many miles, or climb so many stairs, especially when accompanied by scores of eager townsfolk. But gratitude to little Philomena always won the day. She conquered her fatigue, overcame her shyness, obeyed orders and was rewarded by a peace and joy such as she had never before experienced.

Then presently came the day of departure for Naples. Enthusiastic crowds gathered about Pauline's carriage, loud in their admiration of the life-size statue of Philomena she was taking back to Lyons. The French lady must return soon, they insisted. She must remember them in her prayers, too, and help to promote Philomena's cause.

107

Pauline's eyes filled with happy tears as she looked about at her many new friends. "Of course!" she exclaimed. "How could I do anything else?"

Marie Melquiond gave Father Rousselon a quick smile. What a difference between the heartbreaking day of their arrival— worn, travelstained and anxious—and the present cheerful scene! Now it was only Philomena's statue, carefully wrapped against breakage, which must claim their constant attention instead of an invalid at the point of death.

"Father, we can never thank God enough for all that's happened," she murmured.

The priest assented. "Yes, and the trip's not over yet, Marie. There'll be many more good things to come. Wait and see."

Soon these words proved true. As the travelers' carriage proceeded to Naples, stopping here and there to change horses, cheering crowds came out to greet them and to shower them with flowers. Word of the miracle had arrived long ago, of course, but here was the French lady herself. And with a beautiful statue of the little saint, too!

"Tell us all about everything!" they begged.

By now Pauline was accustomed to such requests, and willingly related what had happened at Mugnano. She also brought out a prized possession, a new relic of Saint Philomena, and smiled happily as the people knelt reverently before it. However, it was at Naples that a really overwhelming reception took place. Here both the Bishop and the Papal Nuncio received the travelers in special audience, and presented the city's most precious relic—the blood of Saint Januarius— for their veneration. And as usual there were cheers, speeches and general merrymaking.

Pauline had now entered fully into the spirit of the celebration. How good to be a living proof of Philomena's great power with God! To find everyone so interested in the little Roman martyr! To be going home to friends and family with better health than she had known in years! Why, if all went well—

"Yes," agreed the Papal Nuncio, reading her thoughts, "you *will* do great things for souls, Mademoiselle. God has made use of you already, and He will make use of you again. But there will be crosses, too. Never fear."

Pauline's eyes clouded. "*Crosses,* Your Excellency?"

"Yes, many crosses. Something tells me you will need much courage to meet God's future demands."

These words sent a momentary chill through Pauline's heart. But the day was such a beautiful one, the crowds so eager and joyful, that she put all anxiety aside. Indeed, only one thing seemed to matter now, and that was to reach Rome as quickly as possible.

"How surprised the Holy Father's going to be to find me alive and well!" she thought happily. "And Mother Barat, too."

Needless to say, Pope Gregory was astonished when Pauline arrived at the Vatican, knelt for his blessing, then briefly related the story of her cure.

"Child, it *can't* be!" he exclaimed. "Why, only a few short weeks ago you were ready for the grave! I saw that with my own eyes."

Pauline nodded cheerfully. "Yes, Your Holiness, but it's true! Philomena did cure me, just as I've told you. Now, would it be all right to have a chapel built in her honor at

Lyons? You see, before I left Mugnano I promised her I'd try to do just that."

The Pope smiled. "Of course. And I'm not forgetting my own promise either. We'll start an immediate study of her cause. But first, tell me more about your cure."

With childlike enthusiasm Pauline related further details of the miracle, while the Holy Father and his officials listened attentively. Then presently the pontiff rose to his feet.

"My dear, I believe everything you've told me," he said, smiling. "But we do have to make sure about a first-class miracle, you know. Come, now. Let me see you walk."

Eagerly Pauline crossed from one side of the audience chamber to the other. Then, as the Holy Father motioned her to pass before him through the doorway, she started down the hall outside. Immediately Pope Gregory prepared to follow, accompanied by his attendants. But when Pauline had walked briskly about several of the great rooms, her eyes bright with excitement, an anxious master of ceremonies overtook her.

"Mademoiselle, it's a breach of etiquette to turn your back on the Holy Father," he whispered. "Please . . . you have already done it more than once. . . ."

Confused, Pauline came to an abrupt halt. "Oh, I'm sorry, Monsignor! I . . . I should have remembered!"

But Pope Gregory had caught what was being said, and would hear no word of apology. "That's all right," he told the Monsignor. "It's all my fault. God has already made other exceptions in her favor—and much greater ones." Then, in kind and fatherly tones: "Come, child. Tell me once again about your trip to Mugnano."

CHAPTER 19

BACK TO LYONS

The days that followed were full of happy events. Accompanied by Marie, Pauline went on pilgrimage from one historic shrine to another, marveling at all the beauty and grandeur of the Eternal City. She made many new friends, too, including the Master General of the Dominican Order, who readily gave permission for the associates of the Living Rosary to be affiliated with Saint Dominic's family. This favor made Pauline very happy, for since girlhood she had always had a great devotion to Saint Dominic. What a fighter he had been in the cause of truth! What a champion of justice! Yet with it all, how kind and fatherly. Now, in a very special sense, she and all the other members of the Living Rosary could claim him as a friend and protector.

"Marie, I've never been so happy in my life," she announced one day. "With Father Dominic to help us, how can we fail in bringing France back to Christ?"

Marie hesitated. The courageous Dominic, who had feared neither the ridicule of misinformed Christians nor the weapons of malicious heretics, had done wonderful things for the Church, of course. But at what a price! His lifetime of fifty-one years had been filled with hardships of all kinds. Even

111

good and holy men—Bishops, abbots, princely rulers—had misunderstood and objected to his way of doing things. They had been particularly averse to his sending out his young friars to study in the Universities, then encouraging them to teach there themselves. Religious belonged in a monastery, they insisted, under the watchful eye of a superior. It was a foolhardy and dangerous practice to allow mere boys to wander about the great cities of Europe—making their own judgments, teaching, preaching, writing, and mixing freely with the people.

Recalling all this now—

"I ... I suppose so, Pauline. But on the other hand...."

"What, Marie?"

"Well, Saint Dominic had to suffer so much! And if he's to be our patron—"

Pauline smiled. She had as little desire for suffering as anyone else. Indeed, the recent prophecy by the Papal Nuncio at Naples that the future would bring her many crosses still sent a chill through her heart whenever she thought of it. But since crosses seemed to be the lot of those who tried to win people for God, and since that was the prime purpose of the Association of the Living Rosary....

"Don't worry," she said cheerfully. "I still think Saint Dominic will make a wonderful patron."

Marie said no more. Indeed, as the days passed she found herself remarkably at peace. How good to be in Rome, to see Pauline enjoying the best of health and making so many friends! Truly, by now it seemed that everyone had heard about the miracle at Mugnano and had decided to make a personal friend of little Philomena, too. In fact, it was not

unusual for Pauline to be pointed out, in church and else
where, as something of a saint herself.

"Look! There's the holy lady from Lyons!"

"The one who founded the Society for the Propagation of
the Faith."

"My, how pretty she is!"

"And how young-looking, too!"

"Much younger than thirty-six."

"But why does she dress so poorly? I thought she was
rich."

"She is rich, but she gives everything to charity."

"And now she's starting a religious community."

"That's right. It's to be called 'The Daughters of Mary.'"

"She's opened one convent already."

"A beautiful place in Lyons that she bought with her own
money."

"Just what do her Sisters do?"

"Oh, they work for the poor."

"And pray for the foreign missions."

"And look after the Living Rosary."

Pauline was amused when she heard the rather mixed-up
report about herself, and did her best to correct it. Yes, she
had organized the early work of the Society for the Propagation of the Faith, copying the idea used by a Protestant group
in England of collecting a penny a week from interested
friends to aid the Chinese missions. Then, in order to call
down special blessings on the work, she had also suggested
the daily recitation of one Our Father, Hail Mary and the
ejaculation *Saint Francis Xavier, pray for us.* Later, she had
formed her co-workers into groups of tens, hundreds and

thousands, so that various leaders might more easily keep track of the collections and forward them to the proper authorities. All this had been around 1819, when she had been a girl of twenty. But since 1822 the work had passed into other hands, and now she was no longer officially connected with it.

As for her wealth? Well, through no merits of hers, God had blessed the family's various business ventures, and on her father's death a year ago she had inherited a fair-sized fortune. But she had *not* founded a convent at Lyons. She merely owned a house there where some twenty girls and women were devoting themselves to prayer and good works. True, the group called themselves "The Daughters of Mary," and perhaps some day they would be a religious community, but for the present they had made no vows and were free to come and go as they pleased.

Marie also did her best to straighten out the facts concerning Pauline's various achievements. However, when several months had passed and her beloved friend made no move to return to Lyons, she found herself growing restless. Weren't they ever going home? Father Rousselon had taken his departure long ago. And since Pauline was in excellent health and the work connected with the promotion of the Living Rosary must be piling up at Loreto—

Pauline hesitated when the question was broached. It was wonderful to be living in Rome, and the days were certainly not being wasted, for visitors were constantly arriving in the Eternal City from all parts of the world. Many of them— Cardinals, Archbishops, missionary priests—could be of great help in promoting the work of the Living Rosary, as well as devotion to Philomena.

"I just can't bear to miss seeing one of them," she told Marie apologetically.

However, on May 25, 1836, after a nine months' stay in Rome, the two finally set out for Lyons. And what a welcome awaited them, especially from the household at Loreto! "Mother Pauline" had been a helpless invalid upon her departure for Italy nearly a year ago. Now, look at her! Why, she was the picture of health!

"Yes, Philomena cured me," she told her little family, laughing and crying at the same time. "Don't you remember that Father de Magallon said she'd do just that if we only had faith?"

Naturally all Lyons was eager to hear the complete story of what had happened at Mugnano, to pray before the life-size statue of the saint and to venerate the new relic which now reposed in the chapel at Loreto. Hundreds of visitors came to call, including the Archbishop of Lyons, and Pauline eagerly gave herself to the task of answering everyone's questions. Then one morning, just at dawn, the portress brought word that a shabbily dressed priest about fifty was waiting in the parlor. He was on his way to offer Mass at Our Lady's shrine at Fourvière, but first he would like to see Philomena's relic and to hear about the miracle.

Pauline's heart beat faster. The visitor could be none other than Father John Vianney, the saintly parish priest of Ars! And if he had just arrived, he must have walked the whole night to make the eighteen-mile trip from Ars to Lyons.

"The poor soul!" she thought, as she hastened down to the parlor. "Why doesn't he tell us when he plans a visit? It'd be so easy to send a carriage for him. . . ."

HE WOULD LIKE TO SEE PHILOMENA'S RELIC.

116

CHAPTER 20

THE CURÉ OF ARS

Pauline had guessed correctly. Her visitor was the holy pastor of Ars, tattered and travelstained as usual, and much excited by the news of her cure.

"Child, I'd have come long before this if there'd only been time!" he burst out. "But there's been *so* much work, what with the orphanage and people wanting to go to confession. Quickly, now. Tell me what little Philomena did for you. Then let me see the new relic."

Pauline suppressed a smile. Father Vianney was always in such a hurry whenever he came to Loreto. Saint that he was, he could not help feeling guilty in taking even a few hours from his pastoral duties. Only the fact that he planned to go to confession to a Capuchin friar in Lyons, then ask certain friends for alms for his orphanage, made the present visit possible. So, wasting no words, she began the now-familiar story of her cure. Later, when Father Vianney had returned from offering Mass at Our Lady's shrine at Fourvière and was having breakfast, she added other details—such as the fact that she planned to return to Mugnano in a year or two on a pilgrimage of thanksgiving; that she was going to build a chapel in honor of Philomena; also, that she felt convinced her life had been spared so that she might do something very special for the spiritual welfare of the French working class.

"I don't know what it is, Father, or when I'm going to do it," she confessed, "but I'm sure God has a plan. Will you say a prayer that I find out what it is—soon?"

Father Vianney nodded eagerly. "Of course, child. I pray for you every day, you know that. And for everyone else here at Loreto, too. But now I'll pray extra hard, especially to little Philomena. And I'm quite sure—"

"Yes, Father?"

"That she'll help you right away. After all, she must be grateful that at Ars we're planning a fine chapel in her honor, too. It'll be opened as soon as Pope Gregory allows public devotion to her. Then everyone can pray before the fine relic you sent me from Italy."

Pauline's eyes shone. "You liked it, Father?"

"*Liked* it? Child, it's the most beautiful gift I ever received! Ah, if you just knew what graces have been showered on our little parish since it came. . . ."

For the second time Pauline suppressed a smile. Ever since Father Vianney's arrival in Ars, eighteen years ago, people had been insisting that he was a saint whose words could touch the heart of the most hardened sinner. He could heal sick bodies, too. In fact, because of the countless conversions and cures which had taken place in Ars, the little village had gradually become one of the most famous places of pilgrimage in all France.

At first so much publicity had greatly distressed Father Vianney—to say nothing of all the honors that began to come his way. Then he had relieved himself of the burden

of so much importance by attributing the various miracles to
certain heavenly friends—Saint John the Baptist, Saint Mi-
chael the Archangel, Saint John Francis Regis. Now it was
Philomena's turn to be in the limelight. But few were deceived by his little ruse, Pauline reflected. Most people still
realized the truth. It was largely his own prayers, his own
penances, which touched the Heart of God and wrought so
many blessings for those who asked his help.

Suddenly she recollected herself with a start. Reading her
thoughts, perhaps, and disturbed by them, Father Vianney had
risen to his feet and was putting on his battered hat.

"Father, you're not going!" she burst out reproachfully.
"Why, you've only just come! And there were so many things
I wanted to ask you. . . ."

Smiling, the pastor of Ars shook his head. "We'll save
them for the next time, child. Now, God bless you. And pray
for me."

Disappointed but not much surprised, Pauline followed her
visitor to the door and pressed upon him a generous alms
for his orphanage. But the offer of a carriage to take him
about the city on his errands, thence home to Ars, was gently
refused. A poor parish priest going about in a carriage! Besides, it was a fine day for walking—

When Marie Melquiond heard about the early morning
visitor, she was greatly impressed. "How lucky we are to
know a holy man like Father Vianney," she observed. "And
to think he prays for us every day, too!"

"Yes," said Pauline thoughtfully. "We can never thank
God enough for giving us such a friend."

Soon there was more reason for thanksgiving. In January, 1837, word arrived from Rome that Pope Gregory the Sixteenth had canonized little Philomena. Now public devotion to her was permitted in all the churches of the world, with her feast day set for August 11. At once there was a new stream of visitors to Loreto, and to Ars, too, for as yet the chapel there was the only one in France to be dedicated to the young martyr. Pauline was as happy as Father Vianney over the good news, and humbly grateful for the important part her cure had played in Philomena's canonization.

"Soon we'll have our own chapel to her here at Loreto," she reflected. "How wonderful that will be!"

However, there were other matters besides the new chapel to claim Pauline's attention. The Association of the Living Rosary was prospering most remarkably, and in the summer of 1838, when she returned to Italy on her pilgrimage of thanksgiving, she was able to inform Pope Gregory the Sixteenth that more than a million men, women and children were now enrolled as members—each one offering a decade of the Rosary every day and contributing from fifteen cents to one dollar in yearly dues. The money thus received was used to purchase books, pamphlets and devotional articles for the needy.

"But it's still not enough," Pauline told the Pope. "Your Holiness, I want to do something for the working class in France—something really big. But so far I haven't been able to think of anything worthwhile."

Pope Gregory gazed with admiration at his visitor. What an apostolic spirit this young woman possessed! And how well she was looking, despite the enormous work she was doing in Lyons! Truly, the cure at Mugnano had been a miracle of the first class. . . .

"You'll think of something soon, child," he said consolingly. "I'm sure of that. In the meantime, remember that all your friends in Rome are praying for your intentions."

Pauline's eyes shone. Yes, her Roman friends—God bless them—*were* praying. Mother Barat and her Religious of the Sacred Heart; the Master General of the Dominican Order and his friars; Cardinal Lambruschini, who, as Papal Nuncio to France, had blessed the Association of the Living Rosary when it had been scarcely three months old. . . .

Suddenly she looked up hopefully into the kindly face of Pope Gregory. "You're really pleased with the Living Rosary, Your Holiness? I know you've blessed it once, but you'll bless it a second time, too?"

The Pope smiled. "On the condition that you and all the other members pray for me. You see, these are difficult days for the Church, even here in Italy."

Pauline nodded eagerly. "Of course we'll pray, Your Holiness. That's only our duty. Besides—"

"Yes, child?"

"I've always felt it's a real privilege to be asked for prayers. Perhaps, when I go home, I can write about that in the regular monthly letter to the members."

CHAPTER 21

PAGAN BABIES

Upon her return to Lyons, the idea of asking other people for prayers took on greater importance for Pauline. What a meritorious practice it was! And how simple as well! Even if people said that they would pray and then forgot, all was not lost. Pleased with the humility of the one who had asked for help, God would not hesitate to send a generous reward. As for the human frailty of the forgetful ones— well, that was no barrier to His kindness. He would be mindful of their good intentions. But the ones who did not forget—ah, what untold graces would be coming their way because of their kindness and generosity!

"We'd all be better off if we'd only ask more people for prayers," Pauline told the members of the Living Rosary. "And so as not to forget to do our own part, we might have a general intention to remember all who ask the same of us. Surely such dependence on one another is very pleasing to God?"

These words gave rise to considerable discussion at Loreto. Of course it was true that all prayer was good, especially the prayer of a holy man like Father John Vianney. But when one considered the accumulated merit of less acceptable prayers —the prayers of the ordinary people whom one knew—*and* the fact that their intention to pray, even though it might never be carried out, was also blessed by God. . . .

"Pauline's had a real inspiration," one person told another. "Let's hope she's right about everything."

"Of course she's right."

"Yes. Asking other people to pray for us is actually based on humility. And God always rewards that."

"Still, isn't it all rather unusual?"

"Unusual? Of course not!"

"But who ever heard a priest suggest such a thing in a sermon?"

"Well, not all our priests pray and meditate like Pauline."

"And so the Holy Spirit isn't so generous to them with His inspirations."

"That's right. But what if they'd ask more people for prayers?"

"Ah, things might be different then."

"That *is* an idea!"

"Yes, and one that ought to please God, for it shows how weak we are, even the holiest, without His help."

Busy as she was with all the work connected with the Living Rosary—the monthly circular letters to more than a million members, the careful accounting of funds, the distribution of books and devotional articles in needy parishes—Pauline managed to find time for visitors. Indeed, by 1842 the big house at Loreto had become a haven for anyone with a problem. Missionaries home on leave were always sure of a warm welcome and generous financial aid. The unemployed of Lyons, the discouraged, whether in the Church or out of it, could be equally confident of help.

"I think our Mother's a saint," declared young Maria Dubouis one day. "She spends *so* much time in helping others!"

Marie Melquiond smiled. Maria was a newcomer to Loreto, having been sent from Ars just a month ago by Father Vianney, who had been sure that the little brown-eyed peasant girl, pink-cheeked and sturdy, could be a wonderful help in Pauline's growing household. He had been right, too, for from the beginning Maria had endeared herself to all the Daughters of Mary by her good nature and willingness to work. Now that she had taken over the kitchen duties, everyone wondered how they had ever managed to do without her.

"Yes, my dear, I think our Mother's a saint, too," said Marie thoughtfully. "And yet, she does have enemies."

Maria looked startled. "But how can that be, Mademoiselle, when she's so kind and good? Why, when I see her praying in the chapel. . . ."

"I know, child. But don't forget our Mother is a very intelligent woman—and a beautiful one, too. That's enough to make some people extremely jealous."

"But—"

"She's founded two very important works: the Society for the Propagation of the Faith and the Association of the Living Rosary. Perhaps if she'd been a priest, or even a simple layman, few would have dared to criticize her. But because she's a woman, and a single woman at that—"

Maria shook her head. It was too much to understand. Who could dislike Mother Pauline, or be envious of all that she had done? Why, everything she had—time, money, friendship—was at the disposal of others!

"I love her very much," she said finally. "I'd like to devote my whole life to her, Mademoiselle."

"I THINK OUR MOTHER'S A SAINT."

Marie gave the earnest little girl an affectionate hug. "Bless
you, child!" she exclaimed. "Maybe you will!"

As the months passed, Maria's happiness steadily increased.
How good to be living at Loreto! To be useful to Mother
Pauline and her daughters in various small ways! Then presently there was even more cause for rejoicing when Bishop
Charles De Forbin-Janson of Nancy (who was visiting briefly in Lyons), announced that Pauline had just given him a
fine new plan for helping the foreign missions.

"It's the best idea I've heard of in a long time," he declared. "A real inspiration."

Naturally everyone was anxious to hear details, and so the
Bishop hastened to explain. The new project concerned the
welfare of the vast numbers of pagan Chinese babies who
were being abandoned by their poverty-stricken parents. In
the past, the missionaries had not been able to do much for
these unfortunate infants, since the majority died within a
few hours after being left in the streets, in the fields, or on
the doorsteps of houses. But now—

"Mademoiselle Jaricot suggests that we let the pagans know
we're willing to buy all their unwanted children," said the
Bishop. "Of course the sickly ones will soon die, but at
least not without Baptism. Those who do live can be brought
up in our orphanages." Then, after a significant pause: "Now,
who's to supply the funds for such a work?"

The Bishop's friends looked at one another. Who, indeed?
It would surely take a very wealthy person to buy all the unwanted babies in China.

"Perhaps Mademoiselle Jaricot. . . ."

"No, not Mademoiselle Jaricot."

"Then some of her friends. . . ."

"No, not exactly."

"Then maybe the Holy Father himself. . . ."

"No, that's not the answer either."

Finally the Bishop could no longer restrain his enthusiasm. "Our own Catholic boys and girls will buy the pagan babies!" he declared triumphantly. "Now, isn't that a fine idea?"

There was a faint gasp of astonishment, then a chorus of objections from the somewhat disappointed audience.

"But that's impossible, Your Lordship!"

"How could mere children undertake such an enormous charity?"

"Why, there must be thousands and thousands of abandoned babies in China!"

"It would take a fortune to do anything for them!"

The Bishop smiled and shrugged. "Remember the Society for the Propagation of the Faith and all the good that it's been able to do? Yet a penny a week is all that's required from each member in the way of dues. Well, it will be something like that for us."

Then, as everyone stared in puzzled silence, the Bishop began to outline the plan which Pauline had suggested. From now on Catholic children everywhere would have their own missionary society: the Association of the Holy Childhood. Each boy and girl would contribute a penny a month for the ransom of pagan babies. They would pray for their adopted brothers and sisters, too—one Hail Mary a day and one ejaculation: *Holy Virgin Mary, pray for us and for the poor pagan children.* If all went well, the new missionary effort would produce enormous results.

"Mademoiselle Jaricot's sure of that, and so am I," said the Bishop. "Thank God I happened to ask her for advice."

CHAPTER 22

THE MODEL CHRISTIAN TOWN

Very soon the Bishop's confidence in Pauline's suggestion was being rewarded. Boys and girls of all ages, anxious to do their part for the missions, were joining the Association of the Holy Childhood and even contributing extra pennies for the ransom of pagan babies. Right now, of course, only French children were members, but surely in a little while the movement would spread to other lands? Perhaps even to America, as yet only a missionary country itself. . . .

"How wonderful it all is!" thought young Maria, as she went about her kitchen duties. "Our Mother has actually started a third great work for the Church!"

Naturally Pauline was as pleased as anyone else about the success of the Association of the Holy Childhood. However, the great longing to help the laboring classes which she had had when a girl was still with her. After all, as she had so often pointed out to Father Wurtz, and more recently to Pope Gregory the Sixteenth and Cardinal Lambruschini, how could people turn their minds to spiritual things when they had to wage a constant struggle against the most wretched living and working conditions? Yet no practical solution to this problem had ever presented itself, despite all her prayers and efforts.

"If the Church loses the workers, the Devil gains them," she often reflected. "Dear Lord, isn't there something I can *do*?"

Then one day an idea did come to Pauline. Perhaps she could establish a community of workers herself—a model Christian town—where men and women would be paid a living wage, the children educated, the sick and aged cared for. Naturally it would take a good deal of money to finance such a project, as well as considerable thought and planning, but surely it could be done?

"The town would be centered about a factory," she explained to Father Vianney when he stopped at Loreto for a brief visit. "All the men would work there, and some of the women, too. There'd be a church, of course, with daily Mass; a school and hospital. And every family would have a nice house and garden. But above all, Father, the workers would be paid a just wage. And they'd have plenty of leisure time to enjoy their homes and families. Now—what do you think of the idea?"

Father Vianney was jubilant. "Child, it's wonderful!" he burst out. "Just wonderful! In God's Name, don't let anything keep you from carrying it out."

Pauline blushed with excitement. "Of course it'll take a lot of money, Father—far more than Papa left me. And more than he left to Paul and Sophie, too. But perhaps. . . ."

"Now, now, Pauline, don't worry about money. Remember what we've been able to do at Ars just because we trusted in the Heavenly Father?"

Pauline nodded happily. For years the good priest before her had been conducting *Providence,* his famous orphanage, with no income save what people gave him in alms. He had also made many improvements in his parish church, and the chapel of Saint Philomena was beautiful beyond description. There had been hard times, of course, but in the end everything had turned out well.

"If you'll only pray for us, Father, I'm sure we'll be able to raise all the money we need," she said confidently. "And to find the right location, too."

Other friends, including Bishop Villecourt of La Rochelle, were equally enthusiastic about the new model town. What a wonderful scheme to help the workers! And what a pity that no one had thought of it before! If they had, surely by now many unbelievers would have developed a real interest in the Church? For how true it was that what these poor people needed most was love—genuine Christian love. And since they seldom found it in their employers (even though the latter professed to be followers of Christ), the majority had long since hardened their hearts against religion. It was a luxury which only the upper classes could afford, they said. And a rather stupid luxury at that.

"Well, now Pauline's model town will be changing everything," one person told another approvingly. "Just wait and see."

"Yes. She'll make the workingman happy first, then do something about his soul."

"Blessings on her! If only there were more such practical Christian women...."

"And men, too."

Even though she was convinced that her plan to help the workers was a good one, Pauline did not immediately try to put it into effect. Indeed, for more than two years she continued to pray and think about it, and ask advice. The death of her beloved sister Sophie on March 2, 1844, at the age of fifty-four, distracted her for a time, but by June of that year she had put her grief aside and was concentrating all her thought on the project.

"An apostolate of love among the working class!" she kept telling herself. "Oh, Lord, if I can just do something to bring it about. . . ."

Presently a plan for financing the proposed model town began to develop in Pauline's mind. She would institute the Bank of Heaven, an association of fifteen wealthy friends who would lend twenty thousand dollars each to form an initial capital fund. The three hundred thousand dollars thus received would be invested in the model town, and gradually repaid to the investors as the products of the new factory began to find a market.

Paul Jaricot (who had found a second wife in Felicity Richond some twenty-four years ago), was not too pleased when he heard about the Bank of Heaven. In his opinion it was far too ambitious a scheme, and Pauline ought to forget it. The same was true, he thought, of several of her other charities, especially the one that concerned the group at Loreto. These women might be pious and well-meaning, he admitted, but they were accomplishing no good for anyone.

"Let them either enter a convent or find themselves husbands," he said irritably. "They've been living on your money long enough."

Pauline tried not to be impatient with her older brother. "But I have *so* much, Paul! And if I can help the poor even a little. . . ."

"The poor! You'll be poor yourself, if you keep on giving everything away. Oh, Pauline! Why do you have to be so reckless with what Papa left you? And why are you always concerned about the workers? They'll never thank you for meddling in their affairs. Just ask Felicity. She'll tell you I'm right."

Pauline sighed. What was the use of arguing? For years Paul and his second wife had been opposed to her various forms of almsgiving. Gradually Victor Chartron, her brother-in-law, had come to regard them with disfavor, too. And since Phileas, Laurette and Sophie (who would have done everything to encourage her) were now dead, she was left without any family approval of her charities—a cross that was very hard to bear. Still, when so many good and devout friends were on her side, people like Cardinal Lambruschini, Bishop Villecourt, Mother Barat, Father Vianney. . . .

"Paul, I'm sorry you feel as you do," she said quietly. "Nevertheless, I think I'll go ahead with the Bank of Heaven. After all, there are really only two problems now: where the new factory's to be located and what it's to produce. And I've been thinking that perhaps John Allioud will be able to help me out there."

Paul stiffened. "You're not going to ask *him* for advice!"

"Why not? He's a good, devout man with plenty of business experience."

"Rot! He's an impractical fool. And a bankrupt one, too."

"Paul, that's not fair! I know John's bank in Grenoble

failed, but it wasn't his fault. And ever since, he's been doing his best to pay off his debts and to make a home for his family."

"Yes. And at whose expense?"

"Now, Paul, you know John *rents* those rooms from me at Nazareth."

"All right, all right! At a fraction of their worth. But why does he idle away his time week after week? His wife and sister-in-law found work in the city without any trouble."

Pauline hesitated, for actually the same question had often arisen in her own mind. "Well, John's a very superior type of person," she said defensively after a moment. "And it's not easy for such a man to find suitable employment. But something will turn up one of these days. I'm sure of that."

Paul shrugged. "Have it your own way," he said stiffly. "At forty-five you ought to be wise enough to judge people's characters. But don't say I didn't warn you." Then, in more kindly tones: "Oh, please be careful, Pauline! You see, it's all very well to be generous with your own money, but when it comes to such a matter as the Bank of Heaven—well, taking three hundred thousand dollars belonging to other people is quite a responsibility."

Pauline nodded. "I know," she said quietly. "And I'll be careful, Paul. Very careful."

CHAPTER 23

GUSTAV PERRE

The antagonism of Paul Jaricot towards John Allioud was a constant source of pain to Pauline. "He just doesn't understand the poor man," she reflected sadly. "But if he could see the devotion with which he serves Mass every morning, or hear him explain the Living Rosary to visitors, he'd surely have a different opinion. He might even help him to find work."

However, Paul seldom visited Loreto, and certainly never at the time of Mass, and he continued to regard John Allioud with suspicion.

"Well, I really can't blame your brother, Mademoiselle," John told Pauline one day. "He has every reason for distrusting me. After all, I did fail in business. If it weren't for your kindness, my family and I wouldn't even have had a home these past two years."

Pauline smiled. "Now, John, that's no way to talk. Lots of people have business reverses through no fault of their own. And one of these days. . . ."

The banker hid his face in his hands. "No, no, Mademoiselle, it would take a miracle for me to pay my debts.

"NOW, JOHN, THAT'S NO WAY TO TALK...."

135

And when I remember all the misery I've caused—the poor workingmen who lost their savings because they took my advice . . . the widows evicted from their homes . . . the orphans without a mouthful to eat . . . the young couples who couldn't marry as they planned. . . ."

"Have you tried praying to Saint Philomena?"

"Oh, yes, Mademoiselle. I prayed to her for months. Then suddenly I stopped."

"But you shouldn't have done that, John!"

"Pardon, Mademoiselle, but I think the little saint wants me to bear my sufferings in patience, rather than to seek relief. And yet lately, particularly these last few weeks. . . ."

"Yes, John?"

"Well, the decision has cost me a great deal. For I keep thinking of my family, especially my poor little daughter Jenny, who is just the right age to marry but who hasn't a cent to her name. Ah, Mademoiselle, these days it takes all my courage not to ask Saint Philomena to let me suffer in Purgatory rather than in this world."

As always, Pauline's heart went out to John Allioud. She had known him for several years, and before his bank had failed he had successfully handled many of her business transactions. But how changed he was since misfortune had struck! Why, he had not made a single worthwhile suggestion regarding the location of the proposed model town! Or what should be produced there either. Truly, unless something was done for him soon, he would have a nervous breakdown.

"John, how would you like to have some of your old friends come here for a visit?" she suggested presently. "It might be that's just what you need to take your mind off your troubles."

The banker smiled wryly. "*Friends,* Mademoiselle? Don't you know they all turned against me years ago?"

Pauline was thoughtful. "But there must be at least one person who still trusts you, John. Some decent Christian who doesn't hold a grudge."

For a moment John Allioud stared at the ground in pensive silence. Then slowly he lifted his head. "There's Gustave Perre," he said doubtfully. "The man in Grenoble to whom you've already been so kind."

Pauline hesitated. John had often referred to Gustave Perre as a genius in business, and a holy man, too, but one who had been having a streak of bad luck. He had spoken so enthusiastically of him that she had already used her influence to help Perre in various small ways. But surely, with troubles of his own, Gustave would be in no condition to cheer up his old friend. . . .

John seemed to read her thoughts. "No, Mademoiselle, if ever anyone could help me, Gustave is the one," he declared. "He might even be able to help you as well. With suggestions for the model town, I mean. And of course I know he'd be delighted to meet you, and to thank you for all your good efforts on his behalf." Then, with a sigh: "But on the other hand—"

"What, John?"

"I don't see how, in my present circumstances. . . ."

Pauline smiled. "There, now, don't worry about anything. I'll find a place for Gustave to stay if you haven't room at Nazareth. I'll arrange for his meals, too, if you like. Now,

go ahead and write to him today. Tell him he'll be most welcome to visit you for as long as he likes."

"But Mademoiselle—"

"No, don't thank me, John. I *want* you to see this old
friend. I'm sure he'll do you a world of good. And if he's
a genius in business, as you say, and could help with suggestions for the model town. . . ."

John's face brightened. "Oh, I'm sure of that, Mademoiselle! Remember, I told you that he owns all kinds of valuable
properties, even some iron deposits at Rustrel. Well, apart
from the reverses he had a while back, everything he's ever
turned his hand to has been a success."

Pauline's eyes widened. "Really? Well, then I want to
see him as much as you do. Go ahead and write to him at
once."

So John took his departure, and soon Pauline found herself
in a state of pleasurable excitement. How wonderful if
Gustave Perre could help with the model town!

"It may be God wants him to be our good angel," she told
herself. "John says he comes from a fine Catholic family.
That, together with his wealth and business experience, is a
combination we could certainly use."

Marie Melquiond was equally hopeful. So were Constance
Poitrasson and Victorine Macaire, two other members of the
household at Loreto. By now the appeal for loans to the Bank
of Heaven was producing very satisfactory results, and all
three women shared Pauline's eagerness to put the money to
work as soon as possible. Not only had several wealthy people contributed their allotted sums of twenty thousand dollars
each, but many of moderate means also had decided to invest

in the model town. The interest rate was good, they declared, and there was the added satisfaction of knowing that their money would be used in a worthwhile cause.

"Let's hope Gustave comes soon," said Constance. "He sounds like a fine person."

"Let's also hope he can help John," added Victorine. "That poor man's melancholy is beginning to get on my nerves."

However, weeks passed and Gustave Perre did not put in an appearance. From time to time Pauline questioned John Allioud about the delay, but with little satisfaction. Apparently Gustave Perre was extremely busy. The iron deposits at Rustrel, which he was hoping to develop on a large scale, were claiming all his attention. There were also other business projects to take up his time, as well as numerous charities.

Pauline held her peace as well as she could. Then one day John Allioud did bring news—and most disturbing news at that. There was no hope of an immediate visit from Gustave Perre, he admitted reluctantly, for new troubles had now befallen him. Certain malicious people had conspired to drag him into court on a series of trumped-up charges. Now he was serving a prison sentence at Nîmes—for unpaid debts, of all things!

"Mademoiselle, it's too cruel!" moaned the banker. "Why, Gustave is the soul of honor! Oh, all this is just going to break his heart. . . ."

Pauline could scarcely believe her ears. "But I thought Gustave was wealthy," she protested. "If he can't even pay his debts . . . or furnish bail for himself while he appeals the case against him—"

"Gustave *is* wealthy, Mademoiselle. And his family, too. But of course his enemies made sure to bring their charges at a time when he'd invested all available cash in Rustrel. Now —oh, my poor, poor friend! What's going to become of him? How's he going to bear this terrible cross?"

Pauline hesitated. Well she knew the dreadful injury which jealousy and slander could inflict upon an innocent person. Had not she herself suffered persecution, especially in the early days of the Society for the Propagation of the Faith and the Association of the Living Rosary? Now most of the antagonism towards her had died away, although occasionally there were attempts to revive the ugly rumor that the work she was trying to do was motivated by personal pride and ambition. More serious still, that she was not above diverting the funds of the Living Rosary to her own use whenever she felt the need for them.

"John, I'm terribly sorry for your friend," she said. "Suppose I tried to help him again? You know, I could lend him enough to pay his debts and have a shorter prison term."

The banker stared in amazement. "But Mademoiselle! How can you continue to be so kind? Why, you don't even know Gustave!"

"No, but I'm convinced he's a good man, and that he's been treated most unjustly. Now—how much money do you think he needs?"

For a moment John did not reply. Tears had sprung to his eyes which he made no effort to hide. Then, in a voice choked with emotion: "Y-you're really serious, Mademoiselle? You really want to help Gustave?"

"Of course I'm serious."

"But ... but I can scarcely believe it!"

"Nonsense! Quickly, now. How much does he need?"

John hesitated no longer. "I think a thousand dollars would be more than enough to set him free, Mademoiselle ... and win you a loyal friend for life."

Pauline smiled with satisfaction. "Good. Then I'll write a check today. And you can take it to Nîmes, John, and arrange for Gustave's immediate release."

CHAPTER 24

QUESTIONS ABOUT GUSTAV

In due course Pauline received a most grateful letter from Gustave Perre. Could he ever repay Mademoiselle Jaricot for all her kindness? Of course not! That would be impossible. He could only pray that God would shower upon her His choicest blessings. However, John Allioud had mentioned something about Mademoiselle's desire to found a model Christian town. Now the thought had just occurred to him that perhaps the Perre holdings at Rustrel could be of use. For, much as he hated to part with this valuable property —vast acres of land rich in iron ore, four blast furnaces, a factory, chapel and homes for workingmen—Gustave knew that sooner or later he would have to sell in order to satisfy his creditors.

"Mademoiselle, I feel positive that Rustrel is meant for you," he wrote. "Even the chapel is made to order for a colony of Christian workers, being a place of great peace and beauty within easy walking distance of their homes. In fact, one reason I have hesitated to sell Rustrel before is because of this same little chapel. It seemed nothing short of a sacrilege to let it pass into the hands of unbelievers. But with you, Mademoiselle, there'd be no cause for concern. I know that Our Lady's shrine (for the place is dedicated to

Our Lady of the Angels)would be loved and cared for, and that it would become the spiritual powerhouse for your great apostolate among the working class of France."

Pauline could scarcely wait to inform her co-workers of Gustave's unexpected suggestion.

"Doesn't it sound good?" she demanded eagerly of the community at Loreto. "Particularly the part about the little chapel?"

The women looked at one another in dubious silence. Since they had discovered that Gustave was serving a prison term, their faith in him had been shaken. As a result, this glowing account of the property at Rustrel aroused less enthusiasm than it would have formerly.

"If Gustave is such a wealthy man, and so holy, why doesn't he *give* you Rustrel?" asked Constance Poitrasson bluntly.

Pauline was shocked. "My dear, how could he do that when he needs cash to pay his debts?"

"But according to John. . . ."

"I'm afraid John's been rather confused about some things, Constance. Gustave Perre *is* well-to-do, of course, otherwise he wouldn't own such a fine place as Rustrel. But apparently his wealth is in land, not in actual money. That's an all too common situation for people of the upper class, you know."

Marie Melquiond hesitated. "To me Rustrel sounds like an ideal spot," she admitted slowly. "But wouldn't you have to see it first before you could make any sort of decision?"

"Why, of course, Marie. It's usually very bad business to buy anything sight unseen. Besides, there's something else to consider."

"What?"

"Well, Rustrel hasn't actually been offered for sale. It was only a kindly gesture on Gustave's part to let me know about the possibility."

Victorine Macaire gave a sigh of relief. "Then let's not argue about anything," she urged. "There's really nothing to decide—yet."

Suddenly young Maria Dubouis turned shyly to Pauline. "What about Gustave Perre, Mother? Does he still plan to visit here?"

Pauline smiled at the newest member of her community. "I think so, dear. In a couple of weeks, according to his letter."

However, the two weeks passed, and then several months, and still Gustave did not come. Indeed, it was not until August, 1845, a year later, that he finally arrived—a pleasant-faced man of forty-one, well-dressed, and giving not the slightest indication that he had ever been in prison. The curiosity of the Daughters of Mary was not soon satisfied, for Gustave spent the first few days in seclusion with the Allioud family at Nazareth (the little cottage which had once served as a rest home for Phileas' group of nurses), and so there was no chance to make his acquaintance. However, everyone observed that Pauline herself was well pleased with him.

"He's a wonderfully spiritual man," she told the community at Loreto. "You'd be surprised if you knew how much he loves the Blessed Virgin, and how well she's taken care of him during all his trials."

Presently Pauline announced that Gustave Perre, accompanied by the Allioud family, would pay a visit to Loreto on

Sunday afternoon, after Vespers. Perhaps Constance Poitras son would be good enough to show the group around?

"At last!" exclaimed Victorine Macaire. "Now we'll really have a chance to meet the famous Gustave. . . ."

But Constance was silent and thoughtful. She had already had the opportunity to observe the man briefly on his first day at Nazareth. She had noted his extreme politeness, his polished speech and ready smile, and somehow the impression she received had raised doubts in her mind. He had seemed far too eager to please Pauline. Then, the disturbing way in which the Alliouds had sought to monopolize him, John hanging on his arm and drinking in every word! Even young Jenny, ordinarily very timid with strangers, had been quite gay and chatty. As for her mother and her Aunt Zelie—

"I guess I'm prejudiced, but I just don't like Gustave," Constance told herself. "I wish someone else had the task of showing him about the house."

However, although the Daughters of Mary were not a religious community in the strict sense of the term, they all considered Pauline their superior and faithfully carried out her orders. Thus, on the day appointed, Constance stood at the front door of Loreto and gave the visitors from Nazareth as warm a welcome as she could.

"Do come in," she urged. "I'll show you our chapel first, and then the rest of the house."

Gustave Perre beamed as he motioned the Alliouds to precede him. "The chapel, my dear? Splendid! After a little prayer there, I'll make three wishes—three wonderful wishes that should bring us all good luck."

CHAPTER 25

MORE QUESTIONS

The tour of Loreto lasted an hour or more, and Gustave
was loud in his praises of everything he saw—the chapel, the
beautiful shrine of Saint Philomena, the kitchen where Maria
Dubouis prepared the meals for the Daughters of Mary and
also refreshments for a ceaseless round of visitors, the various
small parlors where Pauline received those who came to her
with their problems, several larger rooms that served as offices
for the Living Rosary, and finally the spacious library in which
Marie Melquiond spent her days dispatching books, pamphlets
and religious articles to needy parishes throughout France.

"What a wonderful, wonderful work!" exclaimed Gustave
as he glanced about this last attractive room. "And to think
it's all part of the Association of the Living Rosary which
good Mademoiselle Jaricot founded!" Then, after a moment:
"But surely the expense must be very great?"

Marie agreed. "Oh, yes, sir. But the yearly dues from the
members help to defray that—from fifteen cents to a dollar
each, you know."

"Indeed! And what is the membership of the Living Rosary these days?"

"About three million."

"Three million! But...but I can scarcely believe it!"

Constance looked doubtfully at Marie. "The figure is right, for we have centers all over the world," she said hastily. "But please don't think we are wealthy here, sir. The money is spent almost as soon as it comes in."

"On books and religious articles?"

"Yes. And for various charities, too. In fact, we spend so much just to run the work of the Living Rosary that Mademoiselle has to pay her two secretaries out of her own pocket in order to make ends meet."

Gustave was beside himself with admiration as he turned to the Alliouds. "Did you hear that, my friends?"

John shrugged. "Of course we heard it. But it's no news to us. We've been living at Nazareth for three years, you know." Then, in a dramatic whisper: "Didn't I tell you Mademoiselle is a great saint, Gustave? Only on the Day of Judgment will people realize all the good she's done in secret."

Madame Allioud and her sister Zelie nodded vigorously. "Yes, she's the soul of generosity. No one ever brings her a problem without receiving help. Isn't that so, Jenny?"

Young Jenny blushed as Gustave turned to look at her. "Of...of course!" she stammered. "Mademoiselle is a... a *wonderful* lady!"

Gustave Perre smiled affably. "And not the only one either, for we mustn't forget our fine little guide and hostess, Mademoiselle...what did you say your name was, my dear?"

"Constance. Constance Poitrasson."

"Ah, yes. Constance. What a lovely name! So sure, so satisfying! Almost like an omen of good things to come."

"You're very kind, sir."

"CONSTANCE! WHAT A LOVELY NAME!"

"Not at all, my dear. Not at all. I speak only the truth. And now there's a favor I'd like to ask."

"Yes?"

"Let's say a decade of the Rosary as an act of thanksgiving for the splendid afternoon we've spent together. You lead, and the rest of us will make the responses."

With mixed feelings, Constance led the decade. Then, after a few more minutes of conversation, she accompanied the visitors to the front door. What a relief that it was almost supper time, and that Madame Allioud was in a hurry to return to Nazareth!

"I couldn't have stood much more," she confided to Victorine Macaire presently. "What in the world can our Mother see in that man? Why, he sets my teeth on edge!"

Victorine shuddered. "Mine, too, now that I've met him. Let's hope he doesn't pay the Alliouds too long a visit. Or bring up the question of the model town."

However, in just a week or so it was only too evident that Gustave Perre had plans. He had now become engaged to Jenny Allioud, and would stay at Nazareth indefinitely. He had also convinced Pauline that the property at Rustrel was the ideal site for her model Christian town.

"Why don't you go and visit the place?" he suggested one day. "It's only about one hundred and twenty-five miles from here. If you take the stagecoach south to Avignon, then east to the little village of Apt...."

Pauline smiled ruefully. "I'd love to go, Gustave, but my doctors won't permit me to travel. They say my heart's none too good these days, and that I mustn't exert myself."

Gustave's eyes widened with astonishment. "But I thought

Saint Philomena cured you of all your troubles, Mademoiselle!"

"She did, ten years ago at Mugnano. But apparently medical men don't believe in tempting the saints. Perhaps you've noticed that when I go up the hill to Our Lady's shrine at Fourvière, I always ride in a donkey cart?"

"Yes. I've noticed. And I've been wondering. . . ."

"Orders, Gustave. No hill climbing. *And* no long trips. Still, perhaps I could send someone else to look over the property."

Gustave nodded approvingly. "That's it. And preferably an experienced engineer. You see, not only has Rustrel rich quantities of iron ore waiting to be developed. There are vast clay deposits, too. That could mean your workingmen's town might eventually produce some excellent pottery. Even statues and other objects for church use. Wouldn't you like that, Mademoiselle?"

Pauline's eyes shone. The more she heard about Rustrel, the better she liked it. And since by now the Bank of Heaven had sufficient funds on hand to cover the initial purchase price. . . .

"Statues! That does sound like a marvelous idea!" she exclaimed. "I think I'll arrange for an engineer I know to go to Rustrel at once, Gustave, and bring back a full report."

However, when the findings of this competent and trustworthy man were in Pauline's hands (and they did bear out the truth of Gustave's many claims), the Daughters of Mary were still far from being satisfied. Rustrel might be an ideal place for the model town, they said, with one of its four blast furnaces able to turn out six hundred pounds of good metal each day; there might be a fine tract of timber, a flour mill, workingmen's quarters and valuable clay deposits. The little chapel of Our Lady of the Angels might be peaceful and picturesque, and date from the fourth century. But since Gustave Perre was involved, it was far better not to have anything to do with the place.

"He's too eager to sell, Mother, and for no good reason," said Constance Poitrasson emphatically. "Please don't trust him!"

"That's right," put in Marie Melquiond. "There's something disturbing about him, despite all his pious talk."

Victorine Macaire screwed up her face in disgust. "I can't even make a private visit to the chapel but that man has to come and kneel right beside me," she declared. "Ugh! It's awful!"

For a moment Pauline was silent. Then she sighed. "My dears, I don't think you're very charitable," she said reproachfully. "Can't you *make* yourselves forget that Gustave has a prison record? Is it fair to be always snubbing the poor man and refusing to see that he's trying to be a good Christian? Really, I'm disappointed in you."

"But Mother—"

"Doesn't he go to Mass and receive Holy Communion every morning?"

"Well—"

"Hasn't John become a far more cheerful person since Gustave came?"

"Y-yes—"

"All right, then. Forget the little mannerisms that bother you so much, and try to treat Gustave as Our Lady would do if she were here in your place." Then, seeing the crestfallen faces of the young women whom she loved so much, and fearing that perhaps she had spoken too severely, Pauline smiled in her usual motherly fashion.

"Now, now, please don't worry about me," she urged. "I really won't be rash or hasty in deciding about the model town. And just to ease your minds concerning Gustave Perre, I've brought this letter from Father Ricard, an Oblate of Mary Immaculate who lives not far from Rustrel, to read to you."

A hush fell over the group as Pauline produced a sheet of paper from her pocket, unfolded it, and began to read:

" 'Mademoiselle:

" 'I have just received a letter from my old and intimate friend Gustave Perre, in which he tells me of your kind interest in him and the influence you may have in helping to settle his affairs. I do not question your own credit, founded as it is upon your integrity, and if you have to answer for Gustave Perre and his family, you need not fear to speak too well of him.

" 'The only crime of which he could be convicted in the law courts was that of having too good a heart. His failure was not his own fault, but that of others who promised more than they could accomplish, and who abandoned him at the moment when they should have supported him.

" 'Give every encouragement, Mademoiselle, to those who are prepared to provide funds and to do business with my good old friend, for they have nothing to fear. . . .' "

CHAPTER 26

PAULINE MAKES UP HER MIND

For a moment no one spoke. Then one by one the Daughters of Mary began to admit that perhaps they had been too harsh in their judgments of Gustave Perre. If Father Ricard could write so favorably about him, especially after having known him for many years, he certainly must have his good points. Therefore, in the future they would try to be more charitable and overlook the familiar ways that had caused them such annoyance. As for Gustave's prison record—well, they would do their best to forget about it, too.

"My dears, that's wonderful!" exclaimed Pauline. "It's just what I've been wanting to hear." Then, after a moment: "There's one more thing, though. How long do you think I've had this letter?"

The group looked at one another in silence, only Victorine venturing an opinion.

"It . . . it just came, Mother?"

Pauline's eyes shone. "My dear, it was here several days before Gustave himself!" Then, amused at the general astonishment: "See? I'm not quite as stupid as you thought."

"But Mother! We didn't mean. . . ."

"That's all right. I don't blame you for being worried.

153

However, when John first came to live at Nazareth and told me about Gustave and all his troubles, I felt sorry for the poor man and decided to help him if I could. But I also decided to inquire first from reputable people in Gustave's own neighborhood as to his character and past record. Well, this is the latest of the many favorable replies I received."

Naturally the Daughters of Mary were now much relieved concerning Gustave Perre. This change of heart delighted Pauline, and she was even more pleased when Father Ricard came in person to see her, and again urged that she have every confidence in his friend.

"Gustave's a good man, Mademoiselle, and belongs to a fine Catholic family," he said reassuringly. "If he's advised you to buy Rustrel, I think you ought to do it."

But eager though she was to begin her cherished project, Pauline still hesitated about buying Rustrel. The place might cost as much as one hundred thousand dollars, and it would take even more to develop it properly. Perhaps eventually nearly half a million dollars would be involved. Besides, her brother Paul and her brother-in-law Victor Chartron would be furious if she actually went against their wishes and bought the Perre estate. . . .

"I really don't know what to do," she reflected soberly.

Then, late in September, Gustave brought disturbing news. His creditors had made a surprise move and were forcing the sale of Rustrel within the next day or so. If Pauline really wanted the place, she must act quickly. And anonymously, too, since it was common knowledge that she was a wealthy woman in her own right, and that even more money was available to her through the Bank of Heaven.

"If your name were to figure in the early proceedings, Mademoiselle, Rustrel's price would soar beyond reason," Gustave declared in worried tones. "But it'd be different if you acted through an agent. That's a very common business procedure, you know, and an honest one, too."

Pauline frowned. "Of course. My lawyers often handle matters for me in that way. But—well, I'm not quite sure. . . ."

"*What?* You don't want Rustrel?"

"Of course I want it! But I'd like to discuss things again with my lawyers, especially the question of who's to be my agent."

Gustave shook his head doubtfully. "There's not much time, Mademoiselle. The sale's to be in a day or two, and it will take nearly that long, even by fastest stagecoach, to get to Rustrel."

Pauline was aghast. "You mean the agent ought to leave —*today?*"

"Yes. Otherwise someone else may get the property."

Pauline's heart sank. How dreadful if Rustrel, with its beautiful little chapel dedicated to Our Lady of the Angels, should go to another purchaser!

"Gustave, come back in two hours," she said with surprising calmness. "I . . . I want to be alone for a while."

Somewhat reluctantly Gustave took his leave. But upon his return, his spirits quickly rose. Although Pauline had been unable to locate her lawyers and other financial advisers on such short notice, nevertheless she had decided to buy Rustrel. And she had appointed him her sole agent to negotiate the deal.

"Mademoiselle, you'll never regret what you've done!" he

burst out happily. "And what an honor that you trust *me* to represent you!"

Pauline smiled. "Why shouldn't I trust you? After all, you do know more about Rustrel than anyone else. Besides, I'm sure you'll try to get the place at a reasonable price."

Gustave nodded eagerly. "Oh, yes, Mademoiselle! That's certainly little enough to do in return for all your kindness to me. As for the money—"

"I have it ready. But please be careful. It doesn't belong to us, you know, but to people who believe we're going to help the workingman and his family."

Slowly, and with great devotion, Gustave made the Sign of the Cross. "Mademoiselle, I'll not waste a single penny," he promised. "Be assured of that. And I won't waste time either. I'll start for Rustrel at once."

Tingling with nervous excitement, Pauline hurried to the chapel as soon as Gustave had gone. The die was cast now, for better or for worse. But surely everything would turn out well? Why, it had to! Of course there was still the dreadful possibility that she had acted too late, and that Rustrel would be bought by someone else. And yet—

"Dear Lord, please don't let it happen!" she begged. "Please let Gustave be in time. . . ."

Naturally everyone else at Loreto was anxious, too, and much relieved when word arrived from Gustave that he had succeeded in buying Rustrel. It had cost some ninety thousand dollars but was certainly worth every penny of it. In three months or so, after certain necessary repairs had been made, the first blast furnace would be put in operation. Then work would start on repairing the other three furnaces. In the spring, if all went well, several acres of rich soil would be placed under cultivation and various crops sown. The mill would also be repaired, so that in the fall the workers would have their own flour for bread. And of course the little chapel would be cleaned and redecorated at once, so that Mass could be fittingly offered there each day.

Pauline was overjoyed. In January the model town would be a reality! Workingmen would be able to raise their children in a truly Christian atmosphere! The little ones themselves would have the chance to learn a trade that appealed to them, and some day establish their own happy homes. . . .

"We'll call the place 'Our Lady of the Angels,' after the Blessed Mother's own chapel," Pauline told the Daughters of Mary, her eyes bright with excitement. "Oh, my dears, isn't it all too wonderful?"

CHAPTER 27

WARNINGS AND REASSURANCES

In January, as he had promised, Gustave Perre wrote to Pauline that the blessing of the first blast furnace had just taken place. There had been Benediction afterwards in Our Lady's chapel, at which all the workers had assisted. Fine quality iron ore was now being produced, and everything was going exceedingly well. Even certain hard-hearted creditors, noting that Mademoiselle had made him manager of the model town, had set aside their former distrust and were now his friends. As for Jenny Allioud, his young bride of a month, how happy she was to be with him at Our Lady of the Angels! And how grateful for Mademoiselle's generous wedding gift of two hundred and forty dollars!

Pauline read and reread Gustave's letter with deepening satisfaction. If only she could pay a visit to her project! But of course the doctors would never permit that, especially during the winter months. Perhaps in the spring, though, when the weather was warmer. . . .

"I simply *must* go!" she kept telling herself. "I'll never be happy until I've seen Our Lady of the Angels with my own eyes—*and* prayed in the little chapel."

Very soon there were other letters for Pauline. They, too, came from the vicinity of Rustrel. However, they were anonymous, and most disturbing in content. Mademoiselle Jaricot was a fool to trust Gustave Perre, they said. This man was an utter scoundrel, and living like a king on money meant to operate the model town. In fact, he had done nothing at all to set the place in order. The workers he had hired were also scoundrels—a lazy, drunken crew—with not the slightest interest in religion. The sooner Mademoiselle discovered her mistake and sent the whole lot packing, the better.

John Allioud merely shrugged when Pauline showed him the letters. "Poor Gustave, his enemies are after him again," he remarked dryly. "What a good thing he still has loyal friends like you and me to stand behind him."

Pauline nodded slowly. "Y-yes, but on the other hand—"

"What, Mademoiselle?"

"Well, I've sent considerable money to Rustrel these last few months. And it could be...."

"Mademoiselle! You're not doubting Gustave's honesty!"

Such pain and shock were in John's voice that Pauline felt guilty. "No, no, don't misunderstand me," she put in hastily. "I only meant that Gustave might have been unwise enough to ... well, to *borrow* something from the funds for his own needs, and so have given grave cause for scandal."

"After he promised you to be careful? And when he knows the money doesn't belong to any of us, but to our friends who've invested in the Bank of Heaven? Oh, Mademoiselle!"

John was so distressed that Pauline immediately regretted she had ever mentioned the disturbing letters. And she felt annoyed with herself, too. People hated to be proved wrong

in their judgment of anyone. What was more likely than
that malicious busybodies, jealous of Gustave's new and important position, should seek to ruin him again? For that
matter, she reflected, if these enemies were so sure of their
charges, why had they refused to identify themselves? Why
had they written to her anonymously?

"John, forgive me! I've been most uncharitable!" she exclaimed remorsefully. "Of course Gustave's to be trusted!
I . . . well, I don't know what came over me to be upset by
these wretched letters. They belong in the wastebasket, that's
sure."

An expression of relief crossed John's face. "Now, Mademoiselle, please don't apologize," he said quickly. "Those
letters would worry anyone, particularly a sensitive and intelligent person like yourself. In fact, I don't think it would
do any harm—"

"Yes?"

"If I paid a visit to Our Lady of the Angels this week and
found out who wrote them. And sent you a complete report
on Gustave, too. Then I know we'd both feel better."

"Oh, I'd be so grateful if you would," Pauline exclaimed.
"And it'd give you the chance to see how Jenny is getting
along, too. John, do try to go to Rustrel if you possibly
can. . . ."

In a few days John did set out to investigate matters, and
soon Pauline was much relieved concerning the model town.
John had written that everything there was prospering. And
the anonymous letters, as he had suspected right along, were
nothing but the product of jealous and evil minds. Truly, no
one could be a more efficient manager of Our Lady of the

THE LETTERS WERE VERY DISTURBING.

161

Angels than Gustave Perre. He had assembled a fine group
of Christian workers and was with them day and night, scarcely
taking time to eat or sleep. Yet busy as he was, he never
omitted his daily visit to Our Lady's chapel to ask her blessing on his work. Naturally he had been deeply grieved to learn
that certain people in the neighborhood were seeking to under-
mine Mademoiselle's faith in him. But he was bearing this
cross with admirable patience. In fact, he was praying for
his unscrupulous enemies as though they were his best friends.

"It's just as Father Ricard said," wrote John. "Gustave is
a real Christian and a thoroughly trustworthy man. I can't
tell you how grateful I am that my little Jenny found herself
such a fine husband. . . ."

Presently Gustave himself came to Lyons on a hurried business trip. "Mademoiselle, we're now turning out some splendid
metal at Rustrel," he announced, "and it's just occurred to
me that perhaps we might try our hand at making medallions
—the religious type, you know—and distribute them to needy
parishes through the Association of the Living Rosary."

"Medallions, Gustave?"

"Yes. Metal pictures of Our Lord, Our Lady, the saints.
Mounted on wood, they'd make very attractive wall orna-
ments. Later on we might also experiment with small medals
for personal use. Now, what do you think?"

Pauline was delighted at the suggestion. "I'd never have
thought of anything like that by myself," she exclaimed. Then,
after a moment: "But won't all this work need some skilled
artists?"

Gustave hesitated. "God has been wonderfully kind, Mademoiselle. Some weeks ago I was able to hire an excellent

metal craftsman, a devout man, too, who'd like nothing better than to make these medallions. The only trouble is—"

"Yes?"

"Well, he's going to need some expensive equipment. And since you've already invested so much. . . ."

Pauline nodded understandingly. "That's all right, Gustave. I knew it would take a lot to put our little town in working order. But one of these days it'll more than pay for itself. So do go ahead and get whatever you need. I'll attend to the bills."

CHAPTER 28

PAULINE WAKES UP

In the weeks that followed, heartening reports continued to arrive from Rustrel and Pauline's enthusiasm knew no bounds. How good God was! And how wonderful to think that still more people were beginning to invest in the Bank of Heaven! Perhaps, in the not too distant future, there might even be other similar projects to help the workingman and his family.

"France has room for hundreds of colonies like Our Lady of the Angels," she reflected happily. "And so has the rest of Europe. Dear Lord, thank You so much for letting me have even a small part in this great work. . . ."

However, the Daughters of Mary were not so optimistic. Despite repeated efforts to think charitably of Gustave Perre, they had never been able to overcome their original aversion to him. They were also worried because Pauline had put such a person in charge of the model town. After all, what did a mere business man know about blast furnaces, mining, the operation of a farm and flour mill? Of course John Allioud had written that Gustave had hired several competent workers. Still, who could trust his opinion either, since he also was inexperienced in such matters?

"But you just can't convince Mother Pauline of that,"

sighed Constance Poitrasson. "In fact, you can't say one word against either Gustave or John. She has implicit faith in both of them."

Marie Melquiond looked anxious. "Yes. Oh, if only she wouldn't send so much money to Rustrel! At least, not until there's been some return on what's already been invested. Sometimes I have the most dreadful feeling—"

"Sssh! Don't let Mother hear you say that!"

"But it's true! That Gustave Perre, with all his pious stories about the saints . . . well, I just *can't* trust him!"

Victorine nodded grimly. "Neither can I. And when I remember how he used to kneel so close to me in the chapel, so that some days I had to be actually rude in order to get rid of him. . . ."

Constance shrugged. "I agree with everything you say," she declared abruptly. "I never liked Gustave Perre either. But— well, what about Father Ricard's letter? *And* his visit?"

The Daughters of Mary looked at one another doubtfully. What, indeed? Father Ricard was a good priest who had known the Perre family for years. He had been most emphatic in his praise of Gustave, both in writing and on the occasion of his visit.

"Well, everything's too mixed up now to make any sense," announced Marie finally. "I guess we'll just have to wait and hope for the best."

Of course Pauline was conscious of what the members of her household were thinking, and her heart ached. How could those who had given themselves to God's service be so lacking in charity, so blind and obstinate?, she wondered at first. But gradually she began to be uneasy in her own mind, too.

And it was not long before there were signs that this uneasiness was not groundless. From reputable sources she now learned that Gustave Perre was being seen in the company of a man named Balleydier, well known to be a scoundrel. He was likewise on friendly terms with a man named Gaufridy, also of doubtful reputation. Both were frequent visitors to Our Lady of the Angels, and their conduct there was anything but becoming.

"I don't like this," she reflected anxiously. "I don't like it at all. I must write to Gustave at once and tell him so."

However, Pauline's letter did not have the desired effect. Gustave replied promptly, and in rather pompous tones, that he was merely trying to practice charity, especially where Balleydier was concerned. This poor man had few friends, was misunderstood and calumniated much as he himself had once been. Gaufridy, too, was the target for considerable malicious gossip. Wasn't it the Christian thing to do to be kind to such unfortunate souls? If Mademoiselle would refer to the first epistle of Saint John, chapter 3, verse 18, she would find proof for this in the following inspired words:

> My little children, let us not love in word,
> nor in tongue, but in deed and truth.

And again in chapter 4, verse 20:

> If any man say, I love God, and hateth
> his brother, he is a liar. For he that loveth
> not his brother, whom he seeth, how can
> he love God, whom he seeth not?

Pauline's heart sank. Gustave's scriptural quotations were edifying enough, but the general tone of his letter was openly defiant. He did not intend to give up his evil associations.

"I . . . I've made a terrible mistake!" she acknowledged,

frantically reading and rereading the letter. "I don't believe Gustave is to be trusted after all. Perhaps even John Allioud—"

Suddenly the whole world seemed to fall apart for Pauline. And when kindly little Maria Dubouis (who never yet had spoken her mind concerning Gustave Perre) announced her opinion that he was a fox and a thief, tears filled Pauline's eyes.

"My dear, I'm afraid you're right," she admitted sadly. "There's just one thing to be grateful for."

Maria stared in amazement. "What, Mother?"

"Only this: that we found out about things in time."

"But . . . but I don't understand. . . ."

"It's all right, Maria. I'm sending no more money to Rustrel. And doctors or no doctors, I'm going there right away to see about a new manager. Thank God, if things do come to the worst, I can always cover the loss with my own money."

Maria scarcely knew what to say. Suddenly her beloved friend looked so worn and anxious! And so *old*! Far older than her forty-seven years—

"Mother, if there's anything I can do. . . ."

Pauline mustered a wan smile. "No, child, everything's going to be all right. We'll put all this trouble in Our Lady's hands and ask her to help us. After all, it is her month, you know."

Maria nodded doubtfully. Yes, it was May, 1846, and Gustave had been at Rustrel only since the previous September. Perhaps he had not been able to do too much damage in a mere eight months. Perhaps, with Our Lady's help, there would still be time enough to set everything right.

CHAPTER 29

HARSH REALITIES—AND NEW HOPES

That very day the blow fell. Pauline learned that some of Gustave's creditors had unearthed fresh charges against him, and he was back in jail. And without hope of an early release either, for now there was definite proof that he was a cheat and scoundrel of the lowest type. Times without number he had successfully falsified his business records, but at last justice had caught up with him.

Pauline was frantic. Was she also to be numbered among Gustave's victims? Had he actually stolen the substantial funds sent to operate the model town? If so, what about John's repeated assurance that everything there was prospering? And the glowing testimonials given by Father Ricard concerning Gustave Perre?

The answers to these questions were not long in coming. John Allioud, basically weak in character, had recently allowed his unscrupulous friend to lead him astray. None of the money sent to operate Rustrel had ever been put to proper use, not even the original purchase price. Everything had been squandered on luxuries and riotous living. Nevertheless, since Mademoiselle Jaricot had appointed Gustave her legal agent and he had signed her name to several important papers, she was now responsible for Rustrel and all the debts incurred

168

against it. As for Father Ricard? Alas, like so many others, he had been thoroughly and completely fooled! The Perres were a good Catholic family, but the priest had never realized that Gustave had always been their black sheep.

Pauline scarcely knew which way to turn. The debt against Rustrel amounted to much more than her own personal holdings. But still more appalling was the amount she now owed to those who had invested in the Bank of Heaven. Hundreds of men and women, trusting in the name of Jaricot, had placed their savings in her hands. Some were wealthy, and could stand the loss, but there were many others to whom the loss would be a tragedy.

"Mademoiselle, you'll just have to ask the courts to declare you bankrupt," Pauline's lawyers told her. "After all, you are an innocent victim of fraud. And once the necessary steps have been taken, you'll be free of every claim."

Pauline's eyes flashed. "I'm not running away from my obligations," she declared indignantly. "I know I've been a fool, but I can still keep my promises to others. Every cent of this debt is going to be paid, gentlemen. And the interest on it, too."

"But Mademoiselle—"

"Every cent, do you hear me? Even it it takes the rest of my life!"

The lawyers looked at one another in dismay. "But that's impossible, Mademoiselle! Even if you did sell Rustrel. . . ."

"Sell Rustrel? At a fraction of what it's worth? That's just what I'm *not* going to do! The place will be what it was meant to be in the beginning—a model Christian town."

"But—"

"I'll put a mortgage on it, and also one on Loreto. Then, with the income from the fine metal goods our workers will produce—"

The lawyers were aghast. "Mademoiselle, that's not at all wise!" they burst out. "Why, even with the best of luck you'd scarcely be able to meet the interest installments, let alone pay off any of the debt!"

"A plea in bankruptcy would be a far better move, Mademoiselle."

"And perfectly honest, too."

Pauline shook her head. "I just couldn't do that," she said abruptly. "Please arrange for the mortgages, gentlemen. And ... and do try to have some faith in me."

The lawyers were reduced to silence. But when they had finally taken their departure, they could not help expressing a reluctant admiration for Pauline's fighting spirit. Certainly this youngest daughter of Anthony Jaricot had inherited her father's honesty and determination in business matters. Why, it could even be that she would make a success of Rustrel, in spite of the great odds against her!

"She'll do it, if there aren't any political troubles to upset the national economy," declared one man hopefully.

"Yes. But of course if that happens, a venture like Rustrel would face ruin overnight."

"That's true enough. And every creditor would be clamoring for his money."

In her heart of hearts, Pauline agreed with her lawyers that she was running a great risk in trying to make a success of Rustrel. But what else was there to do? How could she

"EVERY CENT IS GOING TO BE PAID, GENTLEMEN!"

continue to live in the modest comfort of Loreto when so many people were faced with disaster on her account?

"Maria, you and I are going to Rustrel to look over the situation," she announced one day. "Perhaps things aren't quite as bad as we think."

In vain the little peasant girl repeated the doctors' prohibition against traveling. Pauline would not listen. She must take stock of things in person and also see about a new manager. And she must try not to worry too much about Madame Allioud or her sister Zelie. Although these two women were quite innocent of any wrongdoing, she had felt it best to ask them to leave Nazareth. For in view of her hopes of reestablishing Rustrel and regaining the confidence of the public, it was really necessary to sever all relations with the Allioud family.

"Just the same, I do feel sorry for the poor things," she thought. "And for Jenny, too. What's ever going to become of that unfortunate girl, married to a wretch like Gustave Perre?"

However, there were other things to worry about, especially at Rustrel. Here Pauline found her worst fears justified, for it was only too evident that Gustave had done almost nothing to set the place in order. The little chapel of Our Lady of the Angels was in a particularly ruinous state, and tears filled Pauline's eyes when she remembered that Benediction was supposed to have been given here on the day when the first blast furnace had been put into operation.

"What lies Gustave told me!" she thought sadly. "And how readily I believed them all! Why, I was just as stupid as Eve when she listened to the Devil in Paradise...."

Yet before her return to Lyons, Pauline's old enthusiasm was beginning to stir. The engineer whom she had sent to Rustrel the previous year had not been mistaken in his report that the property had considerable value. Both iron and clay deposits were of excellent quality, likewise the timber and farm land. With the proper handling of these assets, the model town could be a reality after all. And how fortunate that Peter Dubouis, Maria's brother, had agreed to be the new manager and had already hired some reliable men! Somehow it did not seem quite so bad that Our Lady of the Angels was now heavily mortgaged, as well as Loreto; that both Paul Jaricot and Victor Chartron considered her reckless beyond words for what she was trying to do.

"With Our Lady's help, we'll make a success of things yet," she told the Daughters of Mary. "I *know* it!"

Not even the death of Pope Gregory the Sixteenth could shake Pauline's new-found courage. This good friend and benefactor had passed away on June 9, 1846, just a month after Gustave's true character had been brought to light. But in view of the Holy Father's long and prayerful lifetime of eighty-one years, surely he was now a saint in heaven and would continue to beg God's blessing upon her work?

Presently there was another occurrence which Pauline interpreted as a favorable sign. On September 18, according to reliable reports, Our Lady had appeared to two shepherd children—fourteen-year-old Melanie Mathieu and eleven-year-old Maximin Giraud—near the little village of La Salette. And with a most pertinent message for the workingmen of France!

"Our good Mother doesn't like the way they've been doing things," Pauline told her little community. "Especially the fact that so many have been working on Sundays, neglecting the Sacraments and taking God's Name in vain. Unless there's a change, terrible things are going to happen." Then, her eyes bright with excitement: "My, how encouraging it all is!"

Constance Poitrasson could scarcely believe her ears. "*Encouraging,* Mother? But I thought Our Lady was crying all the time she spoke to the children!"

"Yes," put in Marie Melquiond. "Didn't Maximin say she was in great distress, especially about people working on Sunday?"

"Of course, Marie. Maximin did say that. And Melanie, too. That's just the point."

"But—"

"Don't you see how all this makes our model town even more necessary? There, at least, Sunday would be a truly Christian day for the workers. And there'd be no bad language either. Oh, my dears, I think Our Lady's going to take Rustrel under her special protection! After all, isn't the whole place dedicated to her?"

The Daughters of Mary looked at one another hopefully. True enough. Our Lady of the Angels was the Blessed Mother's own town. Perhaps the recent apparition at La Salette —less than one hundred miles from Lyons—was a happy omen that she would help to pay off the debt and make everything a success.

CHAPTER 30

IN DEBT

For the next two years, under Peter Dubouis' capable management, there was encouraging progress at Rustrel. Two furnaces were put in operation, several families of workers established in residence, and enough money made to pay the interest on the mortgages and even something on the debt. However, in February of 1848 came the blow which Pauline's lawyers had feared. Factory workers all over France, long dissatisfied with insufficient wages and miserable living conditions, stormed through the streets threatening violence to the lives and property of their well-to-do employers. The situation was especially serious in Lyons, and Pauline shuddered as she recalled the suffering and bloodshed of the revolts of nearly twenty years before.

"Poor, poor people!" she sighed. "If only something could have been done for them sooner...."

As the weeks passed and France seemed to be approaching both financial and political ruin, the Rustrel creditors were no longer satisfied with the regular interest payments on their loans. They wanted their capital, too. If it was not forthcoming in the very near future, they would have to foreclose on both Rustrel and Loreto.

Pauline's heart sank, for she simply did not have the money. "I . . . I could go about the country asking for help," she told the Daughters of Mary doubtfully. "After all, when it's not for myself—"

The members of the community were aghast. What a thought that their beloved superior, the daughter of a millionaire, should be reduced to begging!

"No, no, Mother!" they exclaimed. "Don't do *that*!"

Pauline herself shrank from the idea of asking for charity, even for such a project as the model town, since she had always planned to have it a self-supporting venture. Besides, on account of the revolution, traveling was not safe. Yet she did have loyal friends all over France, especially in towns and cities where the Living Rosary had been established. And if she explained matters in person, surely they would try to *lend* her what they could. One especially, Bishop Villecourt of La Rochelle, might be able to offer some really good advice.

"I'm going to see the Bishop," she decided one day. "And Maria's going with me."

The eyes of young Maria Dubouis widened in dismay when Pauline announced that they would buy the cheapest seats in the stagecoach and carry their lunch. By the shortest route, it was all of two hundred and seventy-five miles from Lyons to the Bishop's city on the west coast of France. But with a detour south to Avignon, such as Pauline had in mind, plus a stopover at Rustrel. . . .

"No, no, Mother, it's too much," she protested. "You're not nearly strong enough for such a trip."

Pauline smiled. She was forty-nine years old now, and the anxiety of recent months had taken a heavy toll of her strength. But it was certainly impossible to stay idly at home and watch the disintegration of all that she had accomplished; to see Loreto lost to her creditors, as well as the model town.

"I'll be all right," she said confidently. "Don't worry about me."

It was a hot September day when the two set out for Avignon, and more than once Maria's heart was troubled as the stagecoach bounced and jolted over the dusty roads and Pauline grew pale. But there were no complications, and when they finally arrived at Rustrel Maria breathed a prayer of genuine relief. Pauline had stood the trip remarkably well. And how consoling that her own brother Peter was doing such fine work as manager of Our Lady of the Angels! That the iron ore being mined was of excellent quality, and that the model town would yet be a success if only enough money could be raised to pay the debt against it!

Pauline was more relieved than she would admit that she had arrived without mishap. And of all that she saw at Rustrel, she was especially pleased with the two fine medallions which Peter's workers were beginning to turn out—one of the Sacred Heart, the other of the Immaculate Heart of Mary.

"Maria, these would bring a good price anywhere," she declared. "I'm going to take along two samples to show people the type of work we can do here—*if* we can get enough money to keep the place going."

On the trip westward through France to La Rochelle, the medallions were examined with much pleasure by the people who saw them. The members of the Living Rosary were especially enthusiastic, and frequently Pauline was overwhelmed at the kind and friendly treatment accorded her in the places where groups had been established. Several loans were made in favor of Rustrel, as well as a generous promise of prayers. But of course there were also difficulties. Traveling by stagecoach was an exhausting affair, especially in the cheapest seats. Most of the time sleep was impossible. The food, too, was far from adequate—chiefly bread, fruit and very weak coffee.

"It's all right, dear," Pauline reassured her young companion cheerfully. "I'd really feel much worse if we gave in to ourselves and bought any luxuries. You see, we mustn't forget about the debt."

Maria managed to smile. "Oh, no, Mother. That's the most important thing in our lives now."

However, by the time they arrived at La Rochelle, Pauline was deeply discouraged. She was *so* tired! And the task before her was so enormous! Perhaps Bishop Villecourt would have no suggestions to make after all. Perhaps he would be so thoroughly disgusted with her stupidity in trusting Gustave Perre that he would feel justified in refusing all help.

But the Bishop was kindness itself. Pauline was not to be discouraged, he said. And she must not give up the idea of promoting the model town. But it was foolish, he thought, to pay off the debt by borrowing fresh funds which she must attempt to repay later on. No, any sums given her now were to be considered as outright gifts to a worthy charity. By all means she must set out on a tour of France as soon as possible and explain her needs. And she must get the Society for the Propagation of the Faith to help her, too.

"Go to Paris, and talk to the President and his Council," urged the Bishop. "Remind these gentlemen that it was you who founded the Society in the first place. Why, the debt could be paid quite easily if they'd mention your need in the circular letter they send out from time to time. Just a few pennies from each member, and all your troubles would be over."

Pauline's eyes clouded. "But Your Excellency! I haven't had anything to do with the Society in nearly twenty-six years. I don't see how I could possibly put myself forward now. . . ."

The Bishop smiled. Well he remembered the reason for Pauline's withdrawal from the work she had started. It had been practically taken from her in May, 1822, by the unscrupulous Father Inglesi and his well-meaning but ignorant lay helpers. Thanks be to God, the movement had prospered just the same. Indeed, if the Propagation of the Faith had not been turned into a worldwide organization to help all missionary activities, rather than remain a small group pledged to assist the Chinese missions alone, it might not now be enjoying such success. Still, there was no denying that Pauline was actually the foundress, and that she had originated the idea of collecting pennies from groups of tens, hundreds and thousands.

"Forget about the past and go to see the President and his Council," the Bishop repeated kindly. "I'm sure you'll find them more than willing to cooperate. And to make things easier, I'll give you a letter of recommendation to take with you."

Tears of gratitude sprang to Pauline's eyes. What a good friend she had in Bishop Villecourt! And what a practical suggestion he had just made! Truly, the long and difficult trip to La Rochelle had been worthwhile after all.

CHAPTER 31

THE SOCIETY FOR THE
PROPAGATION OF THE FAITH

When Pauline returned to Loreto to make plans for her Paris trip, she found her household reduced to twelve. The reason? In view of the catastrophe at Rustrel, certain of the Daughters of Mary had now decided that their little group had scant hope of ever being a religious community in the strict sense of the term, and so they had gone to enter various convents. But the twelve who had remained were as loyal and devoted as ever . . . even lighthearted when Pauline expressed her anxiety as to how they were going to support themselves while she was away in Paris—perhaps for a year or more.

"Why, we're young and strong, Mother. We'll take in washing," said Victorine cheerfully.

"And sewing, too," declared Marie Melquiond. "There's not the least need to worry about us."

Pauline's eyes shone. How good it was to be at home! To feel herself loved and trusted by these loyal friends who were still not afraid to cast in their lot with hers!

"God bless you!" she exclaimed. "You're simply wonderful! And Julia will think so, too, when she comes."

The Daughters of Mary looked at her curiously. "*Julia,* Mother? Who's she?"

Pauline lost no time in explaining. Julia Maurin was a young woman of twenty-six whom she had met on the recent trip to La Rochelle. Formerly a governess but now possessed of independent means following the death of her parents, she had become greatly interested in the experiment at Rustrel and had volunteered to help in collecting funds.

"She first saw Maria and me in church and wondered who we were," Pauline told her little family. "Later, she went to see Bishop Villecourt and described us to him. He guessed whom she meant, gave her our address, and—well, now we have a new friend. A wonderful new friend. She's agreed to meet me in Paris whenever I wish."

The Daughters of Mary were overjoyed at the good news, and when Pauline and Maria Dubouis finally set out for Paris in June of the following year, 1849, they sent Julia their best wishes. They also promised to pray that the begging trip would be successful, and especially that the Society for the Propagation of the Faith would lend its full support.

"Bishop Villecourt is right," they told one another. "If the members of the Society will just give our Mother a few pennies each, she'll be able to pay off the debt in no time."

Arrived in Paris, Pauline immediately went to see Mother Madeleine Sophie Barat, the foundress of the Religious of the Sacred Heart who had been so kind to her in Rome fourteen years ago when illness had forced her to interrupt her pilgrimage to Saint Philomena's tomb. But although Mother Barat was delighted to see her again, and insisted that both Pauline and Maria make her convent their headquarters, she could scarcely conceal her anxiety. How worn and troubled Pauline looked! How *old*! Far older than her fifty years!

And pathetically shabby, too, in her plain black dress and scuffed shoes. . . .

"My dear, if only I could help you with a large donation!" she exclaimed sympathetically. "Why, when I think of your going about this big city as a beggar, it almost breaks my heart."

Pauline was thoughtful. "It almost broke mine, too, when I first began to consider it," she admitted. "But now—well, I'm prepared for the worst, Mother. Insults, ridicule, misunderstanding—I've asked Our Lady to give me the strength to put aside my pride and to bear everything with the proper patience. I've even tried to thank her for any crosses that may come my way." Then, as Mother Barat gazed in silent admiration: "Dear Mother, please don't look like that!"

"But why, Pauline? What's the matter?"

"I . . . I've made you think I'm very good by what I just said. Oh, if you only knew how far I am from that goal! Why, I positively *loathe* suffering! Ever since childhood I've been that way. I've never been able to conquer my desire for nice things. And sometimes when I read about God's heroic friends, the martyrs and other fearless souls. . . ."

Wise with the experience of her seventy years, Mother Barat suppressed a smile. "I think a lot of them must have been afraid of suffering, too, Pauline. But they just kept on trying to say 'yes' to God. And when you stop to think about it, isn't that all He expects from any of His friends?"

Pauline nodded slowly. "Yes. But the saints were so joyful in their sufferings, Mother! They never complained about anything . . . or felt sorry for themselves! While I. . . ."

Mother Barat stretched out a reassuring hand. "My dear,

don't let the Devil fool you," she said kindly. "You're tired, discouraged and very much worried about this interview with the President of the Society for the Propagation of the Faith. But deep down in your heart, although you may not realize it, you're actually saying 'yes' to God over and over again. And in my opinion, that poor little 'yes' is especially pleasing to Him just because you don't hear it."

Pauline stared in amazement. *"What?"*

"Don't look so startled, my dear. That poor little 'yes' is especially pleasing to God just because you don't hear it. It's ... well, I think it's a beautiful gift He makes to millions of people, especially to those who try to receive Him often in Holy Communion. Only in the next world will they realize that they ever had such a grace, and that it atoned for many serious faults."

Pauline's heart swelled. What a wonderful friend she had in Mother Barat! Just as fourteen years ago, this good religious still had the power to lighten the heaviest burden with a few words. . . .

"Mother, you've made me feel ever so much better!" she exclaimed gratefully. "I certainly have been worried about going to see the President of the Society. But now—well, I scarcely mind at all!"

True enough. Pauline was in high spirits when she set out for her interview on the day appointed, carrying with her two excellent testimonials—one from Bishop Villecourt of La Rochelle, the other from the pastor of the Church of Our Lady of Victories whom she had met shortly after her arrival in the city. She was also much encouraged by the fact that some days previous the Papal Nuncio had promised to put

"MY DEAR, DON'T LOOK SO STARTLED."

in a good word for her with Pope Pius the Ninth, to whom as yet she was a complete stranger. (Three years ago Pope Pius had succeeded to the Chair of Saint Peter upon the death of her loyal friend and benefactor Pope Gregory the Sixteenth.)

"I just can't fail," she told herself. "The Society for the Propagation of the Faith *is* going to help me. I know it!"

Pauline was much relieved to find herself greeted with every courtesy at the Society's headquarters. In fact, the President had nothing but praise for the splendid work she had done in organizing the Living Rosary, and for the fine suggestion made to Bishop Charles De Forbin-Janson which had resulted in the establishment of the Association of the Holy Childhood. True, things had not worked out so well at Rustrel, but perhaps in time there would be a miracle of sorts and the entire debt would be paid off.

Pauline nodded eagerly. "With your help and the cooperation of the Council, that's what I'm hoping for, too," she confessed.

A curious expression crossed the President's face. "Why, what do you mean, Mademoiselle?"

In silence Pauline produced her two credentials. "As foundress of the Society for the Propagation of the Faith, I've come to ask a very great favor," she said quietly. "Rustrel needs worldwide help and recognition. If you will make its plight known to your members and ask a contribution of a few pennies from each one, the debt can easily be paid. Then, at least in one small corner of France, the working class will be able to lead decent Christian lives. Later, perhaps, other such colonies can be started, and millions of people brought to Christ."

The President's eyes shot open. "Mademoiselle, did I hear you correctly? Did you say that *you* founded the Society for the Propagation of the Faith?"

A faint flush mounted to Pauline's cheeks. "Yes. A long time ago, when I was just twenty years old. But it's not credit that I'm looking for now, only help from the child of my heart. In God's Name, tell me that I may have it!"

The President glanced at the two credentials lying on his desk. "Mademoiselle, I'm afraid you've made a dreadful mistake," he observed, frowning. "The Society was founded by a poor servant girl in Lyons whose name has been long forgotten. We have information here to prove that."

Pauline's blood froze in her veins. *"What?"*

"Yes, Mademoiselle. Look at this article from our files. It has a short paragraph about our obscure foundress."

With trembling hands Pauline took the article and began to read. Suddenly she looked up, her eyes flashing. "Why, this is absurd!" she burst out. "I am the Society's foundress and no one else!"

"But Mademoiselle—"

"I know the work did pass into other hands later, and that I've not had any official connection with it in many years. Just the same, I did organize things in the beginning. Now, in the name of justice, I ask you to let me tell the members about Rustrel and to ask their help."

The President shrugged. "I'm afraid I can do nothing about that, Mademoiselle, without first consulting the Council," he said coldly. "If you will come back in a week's time, I'll let you know their decision."

CHAPTER 32

BEGGING

Poor Pauline! Here was a blow she could never, by the wildest flight of imagination, have expected. And when, a week later, she learned that the Council had refused to credit her with the distinction of having founded the Society for the Propagation of the Faith, she was numb with shock and disappointment. In fact, her heart was all but broken.

"That means they'll never help me," she told herself frantically. "To them I'm just a scheming, ambitious woman who wants to be made a lot of in her old age. . . ."

Julia Maurin, now arrived in Paris to assist in collecting funds for Rustrel, was outraged at the way Pauline had been treated.

"How can the President and the Council think the way they do?" she demanded indignantly. "Why, everyone knows you're the Society's foundress, Mother! Look at the testimonials from Bishop Villecourt, the Papal Nuncio, Cardinal Bonald of Lyons, the Archbishop of Paris! Is the Council so stupid as to disregard these completely and say that an unknown servant girl began everything?"

Pauline managed a faint smile. "They're not stupid, my dear. Just misinformed."

"Misinformed! How could they be? Mother, I've often heard—and read, too—that it was you who founded the Society. Well, if that's the case...."

"Perhaps you did, Julia. But did you ever hear, or read, that I attended a certain meeting at Lyons on May 25, 1822?"

Then, as Julia looked a trifle puzzled, Pauline began to explain. It had been at this particular meeting, twenty-seven years ago, that Father Inglesi and several of her own associates had decided that the Propagation of the Faith ought to be made into a worldwide affair to help all foreign missionary groups, rather than just those in China alone. She herself had never favored such a plan, fearing that it was too ambitious, and had thought it best not to go to the meeting. In the end, of course, she had agreed to cooperate with the others, and soon had realized that the new set-up would be a great success. But to avoid any misunderstanding, she had stayed in the background. She had let Father Inglesi and his friends assume all the positions of importance, keeping for herself the less glamorous role of collecting pennies each week from one hundred specified members.

"Yes," said Julia slowly. "I know all that. But this collecting of pennies from groups of tens and hundreds and thousands—wasn't that your idea in the first place, Mother?"

Pauline smiled. "My dear, we'd been using it successfully for three years before Father Inglesi came along. Still, since I wasn't at that meeting on May 25, 1822...."

Suddenly Julia's eyes shone with unexpected fire. "And since no one remembered to mention your name in the record, now these stupid people here in Paris think you're an impostor!" she burst out. "That in 1822 you were just another worker for the missions. Oh, Mother, how horribly unfair!"

Maria Dubouis and Mother Barat were equally disturbed. How could anyone deny Pauline the recognition that was so rightfully hers, especially when she wanted it only to further another charitable work? However, they were considerably encouraged when they learned that Pauline was going to campaign for Rustrel just as she had planned. She would stay in Paris for at least a year in an effort to secure funds.

"There are so many wealthy people here," she said hopefully. "In spite of all that's happened, perhaps I'll get some really good donations."

So, while Julia Maurin set out on a tour of Germany, Austria and England, armed with several fine credentials and a list of prominent men and women who might be interested in doing something for the French working class, Pauline began a house-to-house canvass of Paris itself. Usually Maria Dubouis went with her, and Mother Barat always awaited the return of her two friends with great eagerness. If the day had been a good one, Pauline would be all smiles, despite her weariness. She would be only too glad to show the little hoard of bills and coins in her shabby purse. But all too often she arrived at the convent without a word and went at once to the chapel.

On one such occasion, Mother Barat drew Maria aside. "Tell me, child—was it an unusually bad day?" she asked anxiously.

Maria's eyes were heavy with fatigue. "Just terrible, Mother. We walked miles and miles, but there were only refusals. And insulting ones at that. Oh, if you only knew what poor Mother Pauline had to put up with. . . ."

Mother Barat's heart sank at the depressing news. "What, for instance?"

Maria hesitated, as though she would keep all embarrassing details to herself. But as Mother Barat stood waiting in anxious silence—

"Well, this morning we were passing a dilapidated old house in a side street. Mother Pauline was very tired, and so I suggested we sit down on the steps and eat the dry bread we had with us."

"Yes, and what happened?"

"The owner saw us from across the street and ordered us to move on at once. He said he didn't want any tramps on his property."

"*Tramps*, Maria! But didn't you try to explain. . . ."

"Mother Pauline wouldn't let me. She agreed with the man that we had no right to be sitting where we were. So we put away our lunch and started off again."

Mother Barat scarcely knew what to say as she pictured the weary hours that must have followed for Maria and Pauline—the endless miles of walking, the unfriendly faces behind half-opened doors, the sharp rebukes and refusals. Oh, if only they could go about their work in some comfort and dignity! But of course Pauline would never hear of such a thing. All gifts made to her must be used to pay the debt against Rustrel, not for any luxury such as a rented carriage. As for clothes, the one fairly good black dress which she wore on her begging trips, and another, much patched, which she wore at the convent, were more than sufficient for her needs.

"Maria, in all my seventy years I've never met anyone to

equal your Mother Pauline," said Mother Barat earnestly. "Such charity and resignation! Child, I do think we have a real saint living with us."

Maria nodded solemnly. "I think so, too, Mother. And I'll never leave her, no matter what happens."

For a moment Mother Barat was thoughtful. Then she looked closely at the little peasant girl before her. "Maria, tell me the truth. Do you think the debt against Rustrel is ever going to be paid?"

Maria sighed deeply. "Not if Mother Pauline depends on rich people alone."

"Rich people? But they're the very ones who ought to be able to help her!"

"Of course. But most of them are too blind and selfish where the things of God are concerned."

"You find the poor are different?"

"Oh, yes, Mother! They're accustomed to sacrifice. They know what it means to be forgotten and to suffer and to look for their reward only in the next world. So a great many give us their offerings, very humbly and cheerfully, and even consider themselves privileged to do so. But the rich? Bah! Most of them are afraid they'll be cheated if they make God a generous gift."

However, as the weeks passed, Maria began to take a better view of the great ones of this world. The letters of introduction from the Papal Nuncio and other clerics which Julia Maurin had taken with her to Germany, Austria and England had made it possible for her to gain the confidence of many wealthy people. In Europe, for instance, the Duchess of Angoulême, the Emperor of Austria and the German

Kaiser had each made sizeable donations in favor of Rustrel. In England, Father John Henry Newman, the famous convert, had also promised his support. So had the well-known Passionist, Father Ignatius Spencer, as well as Lady Georgiana Fullerton, the prominent writer.

"Things *are* getting better," she confided one day to Mother Barat. "Why, we're even making some progress here in Paris!"

Mother Barat nodded thoughtfully. Maria was right. Some time ago, at the suggestion of the Papal Nuncio, three prominent priests of the city had formed a committee to help Pauline. Their little group was known as "The Mission for the Workingman," and already considerable funds had been collected. Now they were trying to establish a similar group in Lyons, and had even written to the officers of the Society for the Propagation of the Faith there asking for their support.

From the beginning Pauline had doubted the wisdom of this plan, for the Paris and Lyons committees of the Society really functioned as one unit. However, since she was so well known in her native city, and since so many of her friends held important positions in the Society, perhaps everything would work out well.

"The Lyons group could help me almost as much as the one here in Paris," she reflected. "All they'd have to do would be to inform the members about the Rustrel debt and ask for a small contribution from each. *Or* sponsor a drive in the city itself."

But in due course there was a shocking reply from Lyons. The Society's officers could not possibly help in the Rustrel affair. In fact, they had long considered it to be a lost cause. Of course Mademoiselle Jaricot was a well-meaning woman, although inclined to pride, ambition and an excessive desire for publicity. Now, however, she was really going too far in suddenly claiming to be the foundress of the Society for the Propagation of the Faith; in wanting to make use of this time-tested missionary organization to pay off an enormous debt for which she herself was solely responsible.

"We want nothing to do with this misguided woman," was the word from Lyons. "In fact, we'll oppose these useless collections, both here and elsewhere, as much as we can."

CHAPTER 33

NEW PLANS TO RAISE MONEY

Pauline could scarcely believe her ears. It had been bad enough when the Paris officers of the Society had disputed her right to call herself the foundress and had refused their help. But now that her friends in Lyons had done the same, and were even planning to oppose her efforts to pay off the debt—

"Lord, it's too much!" she groaned. "Truly, I can't bear any more. . . ."

Maria Dubouis was beside herself with anxiety. What was going to happen to Mother Pauline now? Overnight she seemed to have aged twenty years. Her heart was troubling her, too, and she had great difficulty in walking.

"We ought to go back to Loreto," she thought. "It's foolish to stay any longer in Paris."

Reluctantly Pauline agreed, and in the fall of that same year, 1850, the two returned to Lyons. But here fresh disappointments were in store. During Pauline's fifteen months' absence, additional members of the Daughters of Mary, fearful of the insecurity of the future, had left Loreto and joined other religious communities. And although Constance Poitrasson and Victorine Macaire still loved and revered Pauline as

194

a mother and were not afraid to share her poverty, now both believed that God wished them to serve Him elsewhere. Soon Constance would be going to the Ursulines and Victorine to the Refuge of Our Lady of the Compassion.

"Children, you go with my blessing," said Pauline sympathetically. "I understand exactly how things are."

Yet even as she spoke, her heart sank. Once her brother Paul (who had died five years ago) had counseled her to send the Daughters of Mary about their business. She had refused, believing that some day she would be able to form them into a real community. Now this beautiful dream had vanished, like so many others. Yet what was she going to do if all the Daughters left? How could she carry on alone at Loreto, sick and crippled, the prey of hundreds of creditors?

Maria Dubouis reassured her. No matter what happened, she and three other members of the household—Sophie Germain, Maria Candas and Marie Melquiond—would never leave Loreto.

"We'll always be your little family, Mother," said Maria comfortingly. "Don't worry about that."

Yet Pauline could not help worrying. Despite the tiresome months of begging in Paris and Julia Maurin's successful tour of Germany, Austria and England, only enough money had been secured to pay the interest installments. The debt itself was still as large as ever. And so, in 1852, Pauline reached a heartbreaking decision. Rustrel must be sold. There was absolutely no hope now that the model town could ever be self-supporting. And what a tragedy that this really valuable property would have to go at a staggering loss!

"IT'S ALL RIGHT, MY DEARS. DON'T WORRY."

"Perhaps for only half of what I paid for it," she reflected sadly.

However, when all details were settled, Pauline found that things were even worse than she had feared. Rustrel's sale had brought only one-third its original cost. Of course this sum reduced the debt considerably. Even so, it now stood at some eighty-six thousand dollars, plus fast accumulating interest. And there was no way to pay this off except by begging.

Begging! By now Pauline had managed to harden herself, at least in part, to the shame and embarrassment of asking others for funds. From time to time she and Maria still set out on trips to various towns to get what help they could. But they were well aware that many good people who would have been glad to give them something had long ago been advised against it by the Society for the Propagation of the Faith. According to the bulletins of the Society, Pauline Jaricot was a schemer, an adventuress, a religious fanatic. Even her own family had turned against her. It was best to ignore all her pleas for help, no matter how touchingly genuine they might seem to be.

The Daughters of Mary seethed with indignation, for well they knew that Pauline's family had never turned against her. True, her brother Paul, his wife and her brother-in-law Victor Chartron had not approved of her connection with John Allioud or Gustave Perre. Then there had also been some trouble over the attempt of young Pauline Perrin, Sophie's daughter, to become a Daughter of Mary. But repeatedly the Jaricots, the Chartrons and the Perrins had offered Pauline a comfortable private income if she would only give up her various works of charity. That she had refused such an offer, believing herself bound in conscience to pay off the Rustrel debt, was no fault of theirs. Indeed, even now one of her nephews (Paul's youngest son Ernest), was trying to figure out some way to help her. . . .

"Mother, how can you bear all this opposition from the Propagation of the Faith?" demanded Marie Melquiond one day. "It's *so* unfair!"

Pauline shook her head. "I'm afraid I don't bear it, Marie. In spite of all that good Mother Barat said, deep down inside I'm really terribly hurt."

Marie's eyes were puzzled. "In spite of what Mother Barat said—why, what do you mean?"

Pauline managed a wan smile. "I'm too tired to go into details now, my dear. But it does have to do with saying 'yes' to God and not having the satisfaction of hearing oneself say it."

At this Marie was more puzzled than ever. And worried, too. Mother Pauline was so pale and listless these days, and walked only with the greatest effort. And she was in an even worse state if she tried to lie down. Then breathing became so difficult that she all but strangled. As a result, she spent most of her time seated in a chair. But never resting or enjoying any light pastime. No, she was always poring over the depressingly lengthy lists of those to whom she owed money.

"All this strain is too much," thought Marie sadly. "Oh, if there were only something I could *do*. . . ."

The other Daughters of Mary shared Marie's anxiety. Indeed, the future now seemed bleaker than ever, for every spare penny earned from vestment-making and laundry work had to be applied against the debt, and some weeks there was scarcely enough left to buy food. What would they do when winter came, with coal, wood and oil so expensive and Loreto such a large house to heat and light?

Then one day Pauline had encouraging news for her little family. She had been talking to a man named Vassivière, the roadway contractor of Lyons, who had suggested a wonderful new plan for making extra money.

"He wants me to build a path for pilgrims going to Our Lady's shrine at Fourvière," she announced. "The way things are now, they have to make an awkward detour around our property in order to get there. But with a short cut through the garden—well, surely no one would mind paying a penny to save that long, hard climb up the hill?"

The Daughters of Mary looked at one another in amazement. A public short cut to Fourvière would certainly be a great boon to the hundreds of pilgrims who went there each day. But who was going to furnish the money for such a project?

Pauline seemed to read her daughters' minds. "Don't worry," she said, and more cheerfully than anyone had heard her speak in a long time. "I know the path will cost quite a lot—at least two thousand dollars—but I'll go begging in the city every day for funds. And we'll spend only as much money each week as we take in." Then, her eyes shining with excitement: "My dears, do you realize what this means? Fourvière is one of the most famous shrines in France! Nearly five thousand people go there every week. And if each will pay a penny to use the new path—well, we'd soon have some two hundred dollars a month to apply against the debt!"

Maria Candas shook her head doubtfully. The path to Fourvière might be a wise investment, but how could Pauline expect to go on a daily begging trip to Lyons when her health was so poor? Besides, there would surely be nothing but opposition from their enemies. . . .

Pauline smiled. "No, I don't think so, Maria. The whole city is very proud of Our Lady's shrine, and anxious that every tourist go there. I just know the Mayor and other officials will welcome any plan to make this easier and more convenient."

"But your health, Mother! Surely, when you can scarcely walk. . . ."

Pauline shrugged. "Nonsense! I'll be quite all right. Our Lady will see to that."

CHAPTER 34

TO ROME AGAIN

Soon new hope had come to the household at Loreto. The city authorities had approved Pauline's plan for a path to be built across her property that would lead directly to Our Lady's shrine. They had also approved the toll of a penny per person. But most important of all, week by week Pauline was managing to secure funds to pay the cost of both material and labor. And though she was still suffering from heart trouble, and painful ulcers on both legs, she did not seem any the worse for her daily begging trips into the city.

On December 8 of that same year, 1852, "Saint Philomena's Passage" was opened to the public. Some two thousand pilgrims made use of it that day, and Pauline's heart filled with joy as she realized that now all of twenty dollars could be paid to some eager creditor. Of course it was unfortunate that Mademoiselle Roccofort, who owned the adjoining estate, should be displeased about the path and had threatened to have it closed. Still, when the whole project had already been approved by the local authorities. . . .

Sophie Germain, the little portress, agreed that there was no real cause for alarm. "Don't let that woman frighten you, Mother," she said comfortingly. "Things would be a lot different if it were her path, and the pennies were coming her way."

Pauline hesitated. "I suppose you're right, my dear. Still, I don't like to think that Saint Philomena's Passage should cause any hard feelings."

However, by February, 1853, there were other things to worry about. Despite the winter cold, pilgrims were flocking to Fourvière in large numbers, and the income from the path was increasing day by day. But every available penny had to be applied against the debt, and finally Pauline reached a painful decision. If she did not want her little family to starve (or freeze in Loreto's icy rooms), she would have to accept relief from the parish.

Naturally the mere thought sickened her. It had always been distasteful to have to beg for help to pay a debt that was not of her own making. But now to have to beg for herself personally—she, the daughter of a millionaire—to have to depend on public charity for food, clothes and fuel—

Yet this was not the time for self-pity. And reflecting ruefully that at fifty-four she seemed to be as proud as she had been as a girl in her teens, Pauline proceeded to take the necessary steps.

"Well, here's my certificate of nobility," she told her household presently. "See? Father Gonin, our good pastor, signed it."

Undeceived by such a show of lightheartedness, the Daughters of Mary examined the paper which Pauline held out to them. It certified that on February 26, 1853, their superior was in extreme need and entitled to receive relief from the parish.

Maria Candas was quick to sense Pauline's true feelings, and to offer what comfort she could. "Mother, this is really wonderful!" she exclaimed. "Now we won't have to go hungry any more. Or be cold either."

"That's right," put in Sophie Germain soothingly. "And there won't be a temptation to use the money from Saint Philomena's Passage for our own needs either. It can all go to our creditors."

Marie Melquiond and Maria Dubouis made a great deal of this point, too, and soon Pauline was feeling much better. Indeed, as the months passed, the income from the path proved to be as substantial as she had hoped—averaging two hundred dollars a month. Everyone at Loreto was immeasurably encouraged, especially when day after day new names were removed from the creditors' list. And in the spring of 1854, when it became common knowledge that Our Lady was appearing in France again—this time to fourteen-year-old Bernadette Soubirous, a peasant girl of Lourdes—spirits rose still higher. Rumor had it that since February many wonders had been taking place in the obscure little village in the Pyrennees. Apparently, as at La Salette, Our Lady wanted to prove that she had a special interest in the most desperate cases confided to her. And so Pauline's household continued to pray that the debt would be taken care of, so that Loreto would not have to be sold.

"And please, dear Lady, let the Society for the Propagation of the Faith recognize our Mother as its foundress," begged Maria Dubouis secretly. "It would mean so much to us all."

Pauline herself, however, found it difficult to pray for this intention. And in 1855, when certain good friends in La Rochelle began a new campaign for this very purpose, she felt impelled to tell them not to bother. What if many wealthy and influential people did belong to the Society? Long ago, through lies and slander, the majority had been turned against her.

Yet Count de Brémond, who was in charge of the campaign, was not to be dissuaded, and in April, 1856, he began circulating his appeal. However, the disgruntled officers of the Society for the Propagation of the Faith immediately began an appeal of their own. No attention should be paid to Mademoiselle Jaricot's new attempt to set herself up as foundress of the Society, they said. This stubborn and misguided woman, now fifty-seven years old, was as shrewd and scheming as ever. Years ago she could easily have had herself declared bankrupt, and so been legally freed of all financial worry. But no, she had preferred to act the martyr. Now she was out to prey on the generosity of others for still another time.

As the weeks passed, the arguments for and against Pauline's cause increased in bitterness. Throughout France well-meaning priests and religious sided openly against her, for they really believed that she was an impostor. Others were just as emphatic in their statements that Marie Pauline Jaricot was a good woman, even a saint, and that the way she had been treated was a scandal against Christian charity.

Pauline suffered intensely on finding herself the center of so much controversy, and tried to take courage in the realization that this trial would not pass without merit if she bore it patiently. Indeed, for many years she had felt that her poverty, the lies and persecution and physical infirmities, were all part of the Divine plan. They were the price God was asking from her for the success of the Society for the Propagation of the Faith and the Association of the Living

Rosary. If she accepted her crosses bravely, both groups would continue to do enormous good. And the Association of the Holy Childhood, too. But if she tried to escape her suffering, if she let resentment enter her heart and remain there—

"Dear Lord, I've never learned how to suffer well," she often prayed. "Please help me...."

However, in the late summer of 1856, there was news that almost broke Pauline's heart. A group of pilgrims, returning to Lyons from Rome, reported that Pope Pius the Ninth was not at all pleased with Count de Brémond and the other friends who had been trying to help her. In fact, he thoroughly disapproved of their plan to establish Marie Pauline Jaricot in the public eye as the foundress of the Society for the Propagation of the Faith so that she might collect from the members enough funds to pay her debts.

"Maria, this is too much!" Pauline burst out. "You and I must go to Rome to explain things to the Holy Father. He ... he just doesn't know about all the lies and slander...."

Maria Dubouis stared in amazement. "But Mother, the expense—"

"There, now, don't worry. We can find the money some way."

The Daughters of Mary agreed that a trip to Rome was the only solution. It was all very well for Pauline to suffer in silence where her own reputation was concerned. But now that others were involved, particularly such good Christians as Count de Brémond and his wife....

"Yes, Mother, do go and see Pope Pius," they urged. "Explain things to him in full. He'll surely understand and give you his blessing."

CHAPTER 35

A FAITHLESS FRIEND

It was in October of that same year, 1856, that Pauline and Maria Dubouis set out for Rome from Marseilles by boat. Friends had provided some sixty dollars for the trip, but when Pauline learned that she could travel at a reduced rate (being on public relief), she insisted on applying at least forty dollars of this to the debt.

"That leaves us twenty dollars," she told Maria cheerfully, "more than enough for our needs, especially when we're taking our food with us and will be looked after by friends in Rome."

Maria nodded doubtfully. Bishop Villecourt of La Rochelle, now a Cardinal, had written to say that he was providing quarters for them at a well-known hotel. And of course Mother Barat's community would want to help them, too. But what about the return trip? And suppose there should be an emergency of some sort? Surely twenty dollars was not nearly enough to take with them. . . .

"It's all right, my dear," said Pauline confidently, sensing Maria's anxiety. "I'm sure we'll be able to manage."

However, upon arriving in Marseilles, Maria found her fears thoroughly justified. There had been a change in plans, and now the boat that was to take them to Cività Vecchia, a port near Rome, would not be sailing for two days.

"Mother, we simply can't afford to stay at an inn," she declared in worried tones. "Or to buy much food either. What *are* we going to do?"

Pauline was not disturbed. She had an old friend in Marseilles who had often extracted the promise of a visit if she should ever come to the city. Now, she said, they would accept this friend's hospitality.

Greatly relieved, Maria picked up the two worn traveling bags and various bundles, and they set out on the wearying tramp from the waterfront to the fashionable section of the city in which Pauline's friend lived. But her relief was to be only temporary. The maid who opened the door admitted them reluctantly, after an impertinent inspection, and even more reluctantly went to inform her mistress of their presence.

"Don't worry, dear," whispered Pauline, as they stood waiting in the elegant hall. "I guess we don't look very presentable, with our clothes so rumpled from the stagecoach and all these bags and bundles. But we'll soon be able to tidy up."

However, after they had waited some time, the maid returned and coldly announced that her mistress was busy at the moment and could not be disturbed. If Mademoiselle Jaricot cared to return in the evening, she might be able to see her then.

Pauline hesitated. She was *so* tired! And hungry, too. But hiding her feelings as best she could, she thanked the maid and took her departure with dignity. Maria, however, was bursting with indignation when they reached the street.

"We'll not go back to that house!" she declared, her eyes flashing. "Why, that . . . that woman positively insulted you, Mother! And you thought she was your friend!"

Pauline sighed and smiled. "My dear, don't be bitter," she said. "It was all a misunderstanding. Of course we'll go back."

The hours passed slowly for the two travelers. Much of their time was spent in a nearby church, where Pauline prayed long and earnestly for the success of her trip to Rome. Yet despite her best efforts, her heart was heavy. What a pity that Pope Gregory the Sixteenth was dead! He had understood her so well, and had always been so kind and fatherly. She would miss Cardinal Lambruschini, too, the original protector of the Association of the Living Rosary, who had also died. Still, it might be that Pope Pius the Ninth would be better disposed toward her than she had been led to believe. And perhaps the letter which she had written to Cardinal Recanati, the successor to Cardinal Lambruschini, would lead him to receive her without prejudice. Certainly she had done her best to be honest, and to give a complete and unbiased account of her connection with the Society for the Propagation of the Faith.

Towards evening, having lunched on some bread and dried figs from their meager supply of food, Pauline and Maria returned to the friend's house. Lights were now shining from the great windows and there were sounds of music and laughter from the drawing room as the two slowly mounted the wide, stone steps.

"Madame seems to be entertaining," observed Pauline, shivering a little in the chill October air. "Ring the bell, my dear."

Maria nodded, set down the bags and bundles, and gave

"MY MOTHER IS BUSY WITH GUESTS, MADEMOISELLE...."

the bellrope a vigorous tug. But her eyes narrowed when the same maid admitted them to the hallway, then abruptly left them with a few mumbled words.

"Mother, what did I tell you? I just know. . . ."

"Sssh, Maria! It's not for us to judge anyone."

As the minutes passed, Maria cocked her head curiously in the direction of the drawing room. The sounds of revelry had ceased. Instead, a low-voiced argument among several people seemed to be in progress, punctuated by an occasional laugh. At last a pretty young girl peered into the hall. Smiling in an effort to hide her embarrassment, she shyly approached Pauline.

"Mademoiselle Jaricot?"

Pauline's tired eyes brightened. "Yes, my dear."

"Well, I . . . that is, my mother . . . has sent me to say that she is about to have dinner with guests and cannot receive you."

Maria gasped and glared at the girl, but Pauline's control of herself was perfect. Drawing up her tired shoulders, she bowed graciously, then moved toward the door. "Thank you, my dear," she said in a pleasant voice. "Do excuse us for coming here at such an hour. And please assure your mother that we shall not trouble her again." Then, with a little smile: "Come along, Maria. It's getting late."

CHAPTER 36

GOOD NEWS AND BAD

Sometimes when friends, with no excuse, have behaved very badly, one finds kindness where one least expects it. Some stranger comes to the rescue, like a redeeming feature of the human race. So it was for Pauline and Maria. A charitable innkeeper gave them free board and lodging for the time they were forced to spend in Marseilles. And since they could not afford the luxury of a stateroom, the ship's captain allowed them to sit on deck for the entire trip to Città Vecchia. However, the crossing occurred in a thick fog with a heavy sea, and even though the two travelers were protected by bales and boxes piled high about them by the friendly crew, they were drenched with spray by the time the ship made port. And chilled to the bone, too. Nevertheless, it was not long before they were both in good spirits. Cardinal Villecourt offered them comfortable quarters in Rome, as he had promised, and Mother Barat's community was likewise most anxious that they come to the convent for hospitality.

"How wonderful it is to find friends again!" exclaimed Pauline gratefully, after they had decided to accept the invitation of the Religious of the Sacred Heart. "Maria, didn't I say that everything was going to turn out well?"

Maria nodded eagerly. "Of course, Mother. And you were right as usual."

Soon there was fresh cause for rejoicing. Because of an especially gracious introduction from Cardinal Villecourt, Pauline found herself cordially received by Pope Pius the Ninth. Succeeding interviews were equally pleasant, and on the day when the Holy Father announced that he had instructed his Cardinal Vicar to write to the Cardinal Archbishop of Paris, asking him to urge the Paris headquarters of the Society for the Propagation of the Faith to help Mademoiselle Jaricot pay her debts, Pauline's joy knew no bounds.

"Your Holiness, how can I ever thank you?" she burst out. "And to think I was so afraid you wouldn't understand my problems!"

Pope Pius smiled. "My daughter, if the Society pays your debts, it will be nothing but an act of justice in consideration of all the good you have done for the Church. Now, tell me this: Have you sufficient funds for the trip back to France?"

Pauline hesitated. If Cardinal Villecourt or other good friends had informed the Holy Father of the reason she had come away with so little money, he would surely be thinking that she was far more heroic than she really was.

"Well, I'm not exactly penniless, Your Holiness. . . ."

Pope Pius laid a fatherly hand on Pauline's shoulder. "My dear, say no more," he urged gently. "I understand about everything. And since I want you to enjoy these days here in Rome, you must let me take care of all the expenses back to France."

This was almost too much for Pauline. Why, Pope Pius the Ninth was just as kind and sympathetic a friend as Pope

Gregory the Sixteenth had ever been! And to think that he had told her (as well as many others) that he believed the Propagation of the Faith ought to recognize her as its foundress!

"Maria, I feel twenty years younger already!" she exclaimed that same night when a messenger arrived from the Holy Father with a generous gift of sixty dollars. "Now we really can relax and enjoy ourselves."

Maria agreed that everything was going wonderfully well. Not only had Pope Pius overwhelmed them with his kindness and understanding. Cardinal Recanati, the protector of the Living Rosary, had proved himself a loyal friend, too. Then how many missionary priests had come to pay their respects to Pauline! All were loud in their praises of what she had done for the Church. And when they discovered the reason for her presence in the Eternal City, they were both shocked and indignant.

"But of course you founded the Society for the Propagation of the Faith, Mademoiselle!" exclaimed one. "It was in 1819, thirty-seven years ago, when I was just a young man setting out to work in China. I remember everything quite well."

"So do I," put in a second. "Ah, Mademoiselle, if you just knew all the wonders your great work has accomplished through the years! Why, it's helped us to care for thousands of pagans! And to bring about their conversion, too!"

Pauline felt a joy that she had thought was lost to her forever. How good it was to be free of the torture of false accusations! To meet old friends who knew all about her, and to make so many new ones, especially among the foreign missionaries passing through the Eternal City! Then, too, day by day her health was steadily improving, so that now she felt stronger and happier than she had in months.

"It's the good Italian sunshine that's doing it," she told Maria. "Back home we don't have weather like this in November. Now, if we could just stay here until the spring. . . ."

But even as she spoke, Pauline realized that an extended absence from Lyons was out of the question. The three Daughters of Mary remaining at Loreto certainly could not handle her complicated business affairs indefinitely. And so, late in December, after two wonderful months in Rome, Pauline returned to her household.

"My dears, everything went splendidly!" she exclaimed. "The Holy Father's on our side after all. And one of these days I'm sure the Society for the Propagation of the Faith is going to help us with the debt."

Of course the Daughters of Mary were delighted at the good news, and vastly relieved to find their beloved superior looking so well and rested. But it was not long before Pauline sensed that something was troubling her community.

"What's wrong?" she demanded anxiously. "What's happened to make you look so worried?"

Marie Melquiond gave a deep sigh. "Mother, it's a shame to burden you with bad news so soon after your return," she said nervously. "But . . . well, there's no use in beating about the bush. Ever since you went away there's been terrible trouble over Saint Philomena's Passage."

"Yes," agreed Maria Candas. "Mademoiselle Roccofort took advantage of your absence to build her own path."

"And now most of the pilgrims are using it because it's so

much shorter than ours," put in Sophie Germain tearfully.

"And that's not the worst part either."

"No, that wretched woman actually cut across your property in order to build her path!"

"And she's defied anyone to stop her from collecting pennies from the pilgrims!"

"Why, some days we take in scarcely anything!"

"We've complained to the authorities, Mother, but they don't seem to pay any attention."

Pauline could scarcely believe her ears. "But this is outrageous!" she exclaimed. "My dears, there must be some dreadful mistake. Surely Mademoiselle Roccofort would never break the law and trespass on our property!"

But soon Pauline discovered that this was just what her neighbor—an eccentric and impoverished spinster—was doing. And with a display of triumph, too.

"Why shouldn't I make things easier for people to pray at Our Lady's shrine?" she demanded shrilly when Pauline went to see her. "Do you think you have a monopoly on such a good work?"

"But Mademoiselle! You have no right to cut across my land. . . ."

Mademoiselle Roccofort sniffed. "Ah, so you're jealous that the pilgrims are paying me as well as you to go to Fourvière! Well, let them choose between us, I say. That's certainly fair enough."

Pauline's mouth tightened. What an impossible situation! Naturally most of the pilgrims were now taking the Roccofort path, rather than her own, since it was so much shorter. And already this was proving disastrous, for each day meant the loss of a substantial sum which might have been applied against the debt.

"Mademoiselle, I haven't the time or the strength to argue," she said abruptly. "If you won't listen to reason, I must take this whole matter to court. I really can't afford to do otherwise."

For a moment Mademoiselle Roccofort was silent. Then a malicious gleam came into her eyes. "Why, you miserable wretch!" she burst out finally. "Can't afford it indeed! What about that fine house of yours you won't sell at any price? And the luxury of a trip to Rome? Ha, don't lie to me like you've lied to everyone else. You're as wealthy as you ever were."

"Really, Mademoiselle—"

"And people think you're so holy! Well, they don't know you like I do."

"My good woman, if you'll just let me explain. . . ."

"Begrudging a poor neighbor the chance to keep from starving! Listen to me, Mademoiselle Jaricot. Take this matter to court and I'll fight you every inch of the way. Just see if I don't! You . . . you old miser!"

CHAPTER 37

OFF TO ARS

Pauline refused to be intimidated. The whole question of her rival's path to Fourvière was taken to court, and in a few months there was a favorable verdict. Mademoiselle Roccofort must close her path at once, said the judge, as well as stop seeking money from the pilgrims.

"What else did that stupid woman expect?" demanded Sophie Germain triumphantly when she heard the news. "Thank God everything's settled now and there won't be any more trouble."

The other Daughters of Mary agreed. But when several days had passed, and the Roccofort path still remained open, they began to grow uneasy. Apparently their disgruntled neighbor intended to disregard the court order and to collect her penny toll as usual.

"Mother, what *are* you going to do?" they asked anxiously.

Pauline's heart sank, for gradually the terrible truth had dawned upon her. Mademoiselle Roccofort was being backed by the Fourvière Commission! Once this strong and influential body of men (who had charge of finances pertaining to Our Lady's shrine), had been her own loyal friends. They had helped with various charities and had always treated her courteously. But owing to the slander which had arisen against her since she had tried to have herself recognized as the foundress of the Society for the Propagation of the Faith, their attitude was completely changed. The more charitable among them believed she was mentally unbalanced; the others, that she was a scheming adventuress who must not be allowed to live near Our Lady's shrine. As a result (and since they were also anxious for additional land on which to erect a new basilica), the Commission had set itself to acquire the Jaricot property at the earliest possible moment.

"I believe these gentlemen think they can force me into selling Loreto at a low price ... *if* the trouble over the path is allowed to continue," Pauline told her little family reluctantly.

The Daughters of Mary were beside themselves with indignation. "But how can the trouble continue, Mother, when the court has already ruled in your favor?"

Pauline sighed. "The court did uphold my claim," she admitted wearily, "but we have powerful interests fighting against us, my dears. Something tells me that the Fourvière Commission is out to see that the execution of the court order is indefinitely delayed."

As the months passed, Pauline's worst fears were justified. The Roccofort path continued to be used, and there were several anonymous offers (presumably from the Fourvière Commission) to buy Loreto at a ridiculously low figure. Naturally Pauline tried to promote the use of her own path, and to explain her position to the public as best she could. But without much success. Few pilgrims were interested in what seemed to be merely a petty quarrel between two elderly spinsters. They were far more concerned with how to reach Our Lady's shrine quickly and easily. The Roccofort path was the evident answer to this problem, and so Pauline's chief source of income—the penny toll from Saint Philomena's Passage—continued to shrink at an alarming rate.

There were other troubles, too. Despite the Holy Father's suggestion of November, 1856, that the Society for the Propagation of the Faith ought to help Marie Pauline Jaricot to pay her debts, the officers in Paris and Lyons had steadily refused to cooperate. Much as they admired and revered His Holiness, they said, they were not bound to obey him except in matters involving faith and morals. Mademoiselle Jaricot's ridiculous claim that she had founded their Society did not fall within this category. Therefore, they regretted that they could not grant the Holy Father's request.

Pauline's friends were heartbroken. Nevertheless they continued to help her as best they could—particularly the Count and Countess de Brémond, Mother Barat, Mother Saint Lawrence of the Ursulines and Cardinal Villecourt. But in 1858, when the debt had been reduced only to some sixty thousand dollars, everyone was forced to admit that the situation was well-nigh hopeless. By now Pauline's reputation as a business woman had been all but ruined. It was no use giving her anything, people said. She did not know how to handle money.

"No human being can solve her problem," Cardinal Villecourt told Mother Saint Lawrence when he stopped to visit at her convent in Chavagnes. "Everything which has anything to do with it is so strange that one cannot doubt her trials are part of some great predestination of which she is the victim."

Pauline tried not to be bitter over her plight, even though certain anonymous letters accusing her of being a cheat and a fraud all but broke her heart. On the few occasions when she did feel well enough to leave Loreto for a visit with some needy family, or to pray at Our Lady's shrine at Four-vière, there were also those who did not hesitate to plant themselves squarely in her path to sneer and taunt.

"Look at the old miser going to church!" shouted a certain man one day. "You've got to have a penny if you want to walk on her land!"

"Why don't you use those pennies for another trip to Rome, Mademoiselle?"

"Oh, but she wants other people to pay her bills!"

"That's right. Pennies for Pauline!"

"Yes! Yes! Pennies for the old cheapskate!"

"Look at her blush, the wretch!"

"And well she might, the fraud!"

"The miser!"

"The hypocrite!"

Such abuse was more than Maria Dubouis could stand. "Mother, we shouldn't come through this neighborhood again," she declared indignantly. "The people are too cruel."

Pauline, trembling in an effort to keep back the tears, shook her head slowly. "It's . . . it's all right, my dear," she whispered. "All this is very good for my pride."

But in March, 1859, Pauline felt that she could truly bear no more. Bills, angry letters from creditors, the constantly irritating spectacle of hundreds of pilgrims climbing to Our Lady's shrine by way of the Roccofort path instead of her own, the repeated efforts of the Fourvière Commission to force her into selling Loreto—all these were just too much. She must get away from Lyons for a little while.

"Maria, you and I are going to Ars to talk with Father John Vianney," she announced one morning. "A visit with him is what we both need."

Maria looked doubtfully at the sky. The sun was shining, but the March wind had a knifelike edge. Surely the eighteen-mile trip to Ars, even if they did allow themselves the luxury of going by carriage, would prove too difficult for her sixty-year-old mistress?

Pauline shook her head emphatically. "No, no, Maria! I've got to go!" she insisted. "It's been so long since I've seen Father Vianney. . . ."

Eventually Maria threw discretion to the winds. These days Father Vianney scarcely ever came to Lyons, for by now his reputation as a saint and wonderworker had spread through-out all Europe and his time was very limited. Hundreds of people flocked to Ars each week to make their confessions to him and to ask for advice and prayers. Moreover, he was nearly seventy-three years old now, and none too well—

"All right, Mother," she said soothingly. "If you want to go to Ars today, let's go."

So presently the two set out, walking at first in order to save a little something on their fare, and then going by car-riage from Villecourt. But they had traveled only a few miles when a heavy snow began to fall and the ill-tempered driver refused to proceed. The road to Ars was a difficult one at best, he grumbled, let alone when it was piled high with snowdrifts.

"You'll just have to change your plans, ladies!" he snapped. "This is as far as I go!" And quite undisturbed at his pas-

WHAT WERE THEY GOING TO DO NOW?

sengers' plight, he ordered them from the carriage and then set out toward a distant farm to stable his horse.

Pauline and Maria looked at each other in dismay. What were they going to do now? It was bitterly cold, standing on the road in the blinding snow, and in a few hours it would be even worse for then darkness would be setting in. Were they to be stranded all night in this desolate country place? Then suddenly Maria's eyes brightened. She had just caught a glimpse of what seemed to be another horse and wagon coming towards them in the storm. And headed for Ars, too!

"Mother, look!" she cried joyfully. "I do believe it's a delivery wagon of some sort! And yes—the driver's trying to find out if we want a ride...."

CHAPTER 38

A VISIT WITH FATHER VIANNEY

Maria was right. A good-natured baker on his way to Ars was only too willing to give them a ride, and without charge, too.

"The storm'll blow over after a while," he said cheerfully. "Come along, ladies. Don't be afraid."

So Pauline and Maria climbed aboard the wagon, and after a hazardous ride of several miles arrived safely at Father Vianney's house. However, although the trip had been made without mishap, Pauline was now so stiff and numb with cold, and so exhausted, that she could scarcely move. The efforts of Maria and the baker to assist her to the ground were of little use, she was so faint. Moreover, it seemed risky to the baker to try to lift her without more support than Maria's.

"I must be frozen solid," Pauline said, trying to smile. "Maria, perhaps if you went over to the church and asked for help. . . ."

But even as Maria started off hastily, Father Vianney emerged from his house, incredibly thin as usual, his white hair framing a face of almost deathly pallor. Yet his dark eyes were as glowing and excited as a child's over the arrival of his unexpected guest.

224

"Why, it's Mademoiselle Jaricot from Lyons!" he burst out joyfully. "Sister, how did you manage to get here in such weather?" Then, as Pauline made an effort to return this rather strange greeting and to grasp the hand extended to her, the old priest beckoned to a couple of stalwart men passing by. "Anthony! John! Will you give us a little help here, please?"

The men came running, and in a few minutes Pauline had been swung down from the wagon and almost carried into the house. Blue with cold, her teeth chattering, she still managed to thank the men for their kindness, and the baker, too. Then Father Vianney threw open the door of his front parlor.

"It's cold in here, but Maria and I will make a fire right away," he announced. "Come, sister, sit down. Some straw . . . some wood . . . and soon everything will be quite cozy."

Pauline gave a sigh of relief as she looked about the drab little room with its few cheap and shabby furnishings. It was almost as damp and cold in here as outside, but the welcome of her host glowed with the warmth of Christ's own charity. And to think that he was calling her "sister," an affectionate term he had never used before!

"Father, it's so good to be here!" she murmured, settling herself in a rickety chair.

The pastor of Ars smiled and nodded as he hastened to find a chair for Maria. "Yes, but I can see that you didn't come without baggage," he observed shrewdly. "You brought certain troubles with you. Isn't that so?"

Pauline managed a wan smile. "Oh, yes, Father. A whole load of troubles."

"Well, let's see if we can't find some keys to heaven among them, sister. First, though, I must get some fuel. Then you'll tell me your story."

When the straw and wood had been brought in from an outside shed and a fire lighted, Pauline began to open her heart to her good friend, who listened intently. So absorbed were they both that neither noticed when Maria left her chair to kneel before the hearth in a state of mild exasperation. Of course Father Vianney was a saint, she told herself as she rubbed her eyes and tried to suppress a coughing fit. His prayers had worked all manner of wonders. But had he really expected a good blaze from damp straw and moldy wood? Now coils of smoke were rising from the rusty grate and spreading through the room instead of the comforting warmth Pauline needed so badly.

"F-father. . . ." she choked, after giving a futile jab or two with the poker, "I'm afraid that this f-fire. . . ."

Father Vianney looked up in surprise, then got to his feet to peer at the dark hearth. "What is it, child? What's the trouble?"

"The s-straw, Father! See? It never did catch properly. . . ."

Pauline was most embarrassed that her personal comfort should be costing so much effort, especially when Father Vianney seemed so dreadfully frail. "Please don't bother about a fire," she begged. "I really don't need one."

But Father Vianney would not listen. Of course there must be a fire. He and Maria would lay another at once, blowing carefully on the first flames so that all the wood would catch. However, in just a few minutes it was only too evident that such efforts were useless. No amount of huffing and puffing could induce the poor fuel to light. There was nothing to do but to air the smoke-filled room and to ignore its chill dampness while they visited together.

"What a dreadful pity!" Father Vianney told his guests ruefully. "And how the Devil must be laughing. . . ."

Pauline shook her head. There was no need for an apology. She was used to the cold. What she wanted was to be warmed in spirit. "Father, _you_ talk now," she urged. "Tell us about heavenly things. That is what we really came to hear."

So Father Vianney began to talk—about God, His justice, His mercy, the reward of the blessed in heaven. The cheerless little room was as frigid as ever, but Pauline and Maria, caught up in the spell of this rare and joyous moment, completely forgot their discomfort.

Heaven was coming closer with every heartbeat, every tick of the clock, said the pastor of Ars. What a thought, when trials and troubles seemed unbearable! The Way of the Cross was difficult, of course, especially for the poor little souls who tried to walk along it backwards. But what a surprise for anyone who took a step forward, _willingly,_ no matter how short and faltering that step might be! Then, through the hands of the Blessed Virgin, the good God frequently granted one of the greatest gifts in heaven's treasury an _understanding_ of the Way of the Cross, a _love_ of trials and suffering.

"My sisters, our greatest suffering in this life is the fear of suffering. Yet only the first step forward is painful. A child may take it, a poor discouraged sinner, and in one instant be as pleasing to God as some of the most glorious saints in heaven. . . ."

Pauline and Maria sat as though in a trance. How far

away the world seemed now! Even the debt, the trouble with Mademoiselle Roccofort, the lies and slander of the past fourteen years, had faded into insignificance.

"My sisters, to try to get from under a cross is to be crushed by its weight, but to suffer it lovingly is to suffer no longer. Ah, if we could just spend a week in heaven, we should understand the value of our moments of suffering! We should find no cross heavy enough, no trial bitter enough. Then we would run after crosses as a miser runs after money, for nothing but crosses will reassure us at the Day of Judgment. . . ."

On and on went Father Vianney. And as Pauline looked at him, so frail and bent with the weight of his seventy-three years, yet possessed of an inner youth and joy she had never seen in another human being, her eyes filled with happy tears. How good to be here! How truly consoling! Yet even as she rejoiced, a babble of voices was heard in the yard outside and then came a vigorous pounding at the door.

"The pilgrims!" exclaimed Father Vianney, pausing abruptly in the midst of a beautiful tribute to the Blessed Virgin. "The confessions over in the church! I . . . I'd forgotten all about them. . . ."

One glance out the window, and Pauline nodded reluctantly at Maria. The wonderful little visit was over. Scores of anxious men and women were indeed converging on the rectory. It was time to go.

"Father, how can I ever thank you?" she burst out. "You've been *so* kind—"

The old priest smiled as he pressed a souvenir of the day's visit—a small wooden cross—into Pauline's hand. "It was nothing," he said kindly. "Just keep me in your prayers, sister. And take courage. See what it says here? 'God is my witness, Jesus Christ is my model, Mary is my support. I ask nothing but love and sacrifice.' "

For a moment Pauline gazed in thoughtful silence at the little cross. Then she raised it to her lips. "Of course," she whispered, her tired eyes bright with new hope. "Of course, Father. . . ."

CHAPTER 39

PAULINE TAKES GREAT STRIDES
IN HOLINESS

Everyone at Loreto realized that Pauline was in far better spirits after the trip to Ars. Indeed, it frequently seemed that she was scarcely the same discouraged person she had been during the winter.

"Poor Mother! I do believe she thinks Father Vianney will work some kind of miracle and the debt will be paid," Sophie Germain confided to Marie Melquiond one day. "That may be, of course. Still, I just can't bear to see her disappointed again."

Marie nodded thoughtfully. "The latest plan seems to be to take in boarders, Sophie. Naturally that would help some, but it would never settle the whole debt."

"Of course not. What we need is a buyer for this big house—someone who's honest, and who will give us what it's worth."

"That's right. Twenty thousand dollars at least. And a share in the profits from the path, too."

But the weeks passed, and no such offer was made. Nor did Father Vianney's prayers work the much-desired miracle. Not even five months later, on August 4, when his poor body finally succumbed to forty-four years of priestly labor and he entered upon his heavenly reward.

230

"Well, our good friend's certainly not forgotten us," Pauline declared. "And just think! He went to God on the feast of Saint Dominic—our own father and patron. . . ."

The Daughters of Mary smiled knowingly at one another. Mother Pauline had never lost her girlhood devotion to the Spanish friar who had spent himself so tirelessly in promoting the Holy Rosary. Indeed, she all but considered herself a member of his Order, since the Association of the Living Rosary had long ago been affiliated with it.

"Perhaps now Saint Dominic and Father Vianney will work together to do something for us," suggested Maria Candas. "And Saint Philomena, too."

Pauline's eyes shone at the happy prospect. "How wonderful, Maria!" she exclaimed joyfully. "That may well happen . . . *if* we have faith."

But as the months passed, the Daughters of Mary realized with dismay that Pauline was growing less and less interested in temporal affairs. Her heart was troubling her again, she had a severe case of dropsy, and an ulcer on one lung was causing such difficulty in breathing that she had to spend her nights as well as her days propped up in an arm chair. However, it was in December, 1861, that everyone became really alarmed. Then Pauline announced that she was finally resigned to the pain and disgrace of dying a pauper, the debt still unpaid.

"Oh, no, Mother!" sobbed Sophie Germain. "You can't do that. You're far too young to die yet!"

Pauline stretched out an affectionate hand. "Young, my dear? Why, I'm sixty-two years old. . . ."

"That doesn't matter. You still can't leave us, Mother! You can't!"

Pauline smiled. "The good God has waited a long time for me to set aside my pride and accept this last cross," she whispered. "Why should I keep Him waiting any longer?" Then, with a sigh: "I think the Blessed Virgin will help me to die well."

The Daughters of Mary were beside themselves with grief and anxiety. If Mother Pauline were taken from them now, Loreto would surely be sold over their heads. Then what would the future bring—for themselves and for the work of the Living Rosary? Oh, how different things might have been if the officers of the Society for the Propagation of the Faith had not been so blind and stubborn! Then the debt would have been paid off long ago and their beloved superior left to them for many happy years. . . .

"No, my dears," said Pauline quietly. "Don't blame any of those poor people. You see, most of them really did believe that I was an impostor, and so they acted in good faith when they treated me as they did. Now, let's forget about our grievances and start to think of something important."

The four women gathered about Pauline's chair looked at one another doubtfully. "What, Mother?" asked Marie Melquiond after a moment.

"You—I—must become more concerned with souls," said Pauline, "the pagan souls of this nineteenth century and the centuries yet to come. We must pray and make sacrifices for them every day, and willingly, too. That's what God wants."

And then, though her breath was coming in labored gasps, Pauline began to speak with so much enthusiasm of the foreign missions that all were carried out of themselves. What could be a greater work of charity than to bring the True Faith to every pagan nation of the world? Of course not everyone could leave home and family for active missionary life in China, India, Africa, Japan, America. But everyone, even children, could pray for the extension of Christ's Kingdom on earth. And what prayer should they offer? Next to the Holy Sacrifice of the Mass, the Rosary was surely one of the most important tools in the hands of the stay-at-home missionary. Even a single decade—two minutes of loving and prayerful thought on some event in the life of Our Lord or the Blessed Virgin—had incalculable power for good.

Then there was almsgiving. Long ago, when Pauline herself had still been in her teens, God had inspired her brother Phileas with a simple plan to help the Chinese missions financially. She and her friends had worked with Phileas, and in time the plan had been extended to include other countries, where the pennies saved weekly by the faithful had accomplished untold marvels. Indeed, not until the Last Day would anyone realize all the good that had been done by the Society for the Propagation of the Faith. But perhaps there was a growing tendency to forget that the penny offerings should proceed from personal sacrifice. They should be sown in the mission field with tears, so to speak, in order to produce their fruit for the whole Church.

"If I could just make people understand about that," Pauline murmured. "Suffering—it's *so* important! I see it all very clearly now. But when I was young . . . ah, I'm afraid I was far too concerned with the power of money alone. . . ."

Maria Dubouis choked back her tears. "Mother, please

don't say that! Why, you've known suffering all your life! And you've always tried to accept it bravely ... and to get others to accept it, too. I ... I *know*!"

Pauline smiled and shook her head. Then, as a new spasm of coughing suddenly came upon her, she looked up imploringly. "W-where ... where is it?" she gasped. "Maria d-dear, please...."

As the others watched in painful silence, Maria hastened across the room, threw open a bureau drawer and returned with a worn envelope in her hands. Well everyone knew that inside was what the mistress of Loreto had long ago brought herself to consider as one of her most precious possessions. Yet at what a terrific price!

"Here, Mother. But don't you think you ought to try and rest now?"

Unable to speak, Pauline still managed to pry open the envelope and to gaze long and lovingly at her "certificate of nobility"—that single sheet of paper which for nearly nine years had proclaimed her to be utterly penniless, and entitled to public relief. Then, the spell of coughing finally past, she became aware of the anxiety of the group hovering about her.

"There, now, my dears. Don't look so worried. I'm quite all right again."

Maria Candas looked doubtful. "Mother, why don't you put away that paper and try to get some rest?"

"Yes," urged Marie Melquiond quickly. "Let me take it, Mother, while Sophie fixes your pillows."

But Pauline gently refused. "I can rest much better if I have it in my hands," she declared. "Somehow it always makes me think of Our Lady."

"SUFFERING—IT'S **SO** IMPORTANT!"

"*Our Lady*, Mother?"

"Yes. She had nothing in her old age either, you know, and had to be looked after by others. Don't you remember?"

The Daughters of Mary scarcely knew what to say. Of course Mother Pauline had always had a great love of the Blessed Virgin. These days, however, her devotion seemed to have taken on an extraordinary warmth and fervor. A total abandonment, so to speak, like that of a tired child going to sleep in its mother's arms.

"Perhaps that new little book by Father Louis De Montfort has something to do with it," Sophie Germain confided to Maria Dubouis when all had finally left the sickroom. "I mean the one about being the slave of Jesus through Mary."

Maria nodded thoughtfully. "Perhaps," she said.

CHAPTER 40

GETTING READY FOR HEAVEN

Father De Montfort's book, *The True Devotion to the Blessed Virgin Mary,* was not exactly new, having been written in the early part of the eighteenth century. But the precious manuscript had not been discovered until 1842, some nineteen years before, and only now were most people beginning to be aware of the doctrine contained in its pages: namely, that a very sure and simple way to gain heaven is to give oneself and all one's possessions into Our Lady's hands for her to do with as she pleases; to become her slave, so to speak, and through her, the slave of Jesus.

As the cold December days passed, it became apparent that Pauline was becoming more and more absorbed spiritually in the True Devotion. "Mary, my Mother, I am all yours," she was often heard to whisper when she was not conscious of being overheard. And frequently some member of the household, who had come to the sickroom to see if anything was needed, would silently withdraw when she saw the mistress of Loreto gazing in loving ecstasy at the statue of Our Lady of Sorrows which stood in a niche in the wall.

"It . . . it's almost as though our Mother were really seeing the Blessed Virgin," Sophie Germain reported one day. "Just like the saints did. You don't suppose. . . ."

237

"That she's a saint herself? Why, I'm almost sure of it!" exclaimed Maria Dubouis.

"More than that. Some day people will be calling her the patron saint of failures," declared Maria Candas soberly.

The Daughters of Mary were not alone in their belief that Pauline was a nearly perfect soul. Scores of men and women who had remained loyal to her through the years were equally convinced of it, especially those of unusual sanctity, such as Father Peter Julian Eymard, the founder of the Society of the Blessed Sacrament, and Father John Claud Colin, the founder of the Marists. And certain religious communities which Pauline had helped in the early days of their existence —the Sisters of the Congregation of Jesus and Mary, the Clerics of Saint Viator, the Religious of the Cenacle—had never faltered in their loyalty to her.

"How good to have so many people praying for me!" she told Maria Dubouis one day. "Friendship must surely be a little foretaste of heaven."

Maria nodded, restraining her tears. Friendship—the really honest kind—was a wonderful thing. But how Pauline had suffered from false friends! How her heart had been broken, not only by out-and-out scoundrels but also by insincere Christians! Those fair-weather friends who spent long hours in church, but who did not have the decency or courage to stand out against hypocrisy in high places. . . .

Yet as these painful reflections crossed her mind, Maria struggled against them and said not a word. This was not the time to revive such dismal memories. According to the doctors, Pauline had only a few more days to live. And since she had long ago turned all her suffering to spiritual profit by accepting it with childlike faith. . . .

"Yes, Mother, it *is* wonderful to think so many prayers are being offered for you," she said. "Why, it could even happen—"

Pauline smiled. "That I'll be cured? Oh, no, Maria! The last cross is here. I'm sure of that. And I'm *so* glad, my dear! So very glad!'"

With the arrival of the New Year of 1862, the Daughters of Mary realized that Pauline's instinct was a true one. She had received the Last Rites a month before, and had rallied somewhat, but her improvement had not been permanent, and any day now they must be prepared for her death. In order that she might never be left alone, all unnecessary work was set aside. Maria Dubouis scarcely ate or slept, keeping constant vigil by Pauline's chair and supporting her during the long seizures when her breathing became painfully difficult.

"Mother, we really ought to have a fire in here," she declared one night as they sat together in the darkness before the great windows of the sickroom and looked down at the lights of Lyons. "See? It's snowing again. And the wind off the river is very cold."

Pauline looked up weakly from her pillows. "A fire, my dear? For an old woman who can't pay her debts? Ah, no. That wouldn't be right." Then, with a little smile: "How beautiful the city is in the snow! And all those lights . . . they remind me of something."

For a moment Maria was silent. Then, very gently, she began to stroke Pauline's hand. "Yes, Mother. I think I know."

"It's that experience I had as a girl, Maria. The one about the two oil lamps. Remember?"

Maria nodded understandingly. "Of course, Mother. You were praying in church with your eyes closed when suddenly you seemed to see two oil lamps—one full, the other empty. And as you watched, the empty one began to fill itself from the full one. . . ."

With a great effort Pauline raised herself from her pillows for a better view of the city. "Yes, that's right. And somehow I felt that the empty lamp represented Europe, which has been losing the Faith for so long, and the full one represented the pagan countries of the world. Ah, Maria—"

"Yes, Mother?"

"Now I know that I was right! The prayers and good works of the converts in pagan countries will light up the earth some day! But first. . . ."

"But first we must do our part?"

"Yes. Everyone must pray and sacrifice for the foreign missions. Everywhere there must be apostles. Men and women, boys and girls. *Everywhere.* . . ."

CHAPTER 41

THE DEATH OF A SAINT

Late in the afternoon of January 8, the Daughters of Mary gathered for still another time about Pauline's chair. The room was as bitterly cold as usual, but the dying woman seemed oblivious of any discomfort and uttered no complaint. Indeed, by now she had all but lost the power of speech.

"For-for-for. . . ." she stammered, then gazed imploringly at Maria Dubouis whose comforting arms were again supporting her.

"Forgive us our trespasses as we forgive those who trespass against us," whispered Maria softly. "Is that what you're trying to say, Mother?"

Pauline nodded, while a faint smile lighted her face. Then she slowly closed her eyes. At this, Sophie Germain could no longer restrain her tears. "She's dead!" she sobbed.

But old Father Rousselon who was standing near (he was still in residence at Loreto as chaplain), shook his head. "No, she's not stopped breathing, Sophie. She'll be with us for a little while yet."

All that night the vigil was kept beside Pauline's chair. If only Ernest Jaricot could also be here, was the thought of

241

everyone present. Two months before, this young nephew of Pauline's had called at Loreto with the news that he had finally figured out a scheme for paying off the debt. However, since there were still some details to be settled, he had not wanted to discuss his plan. He would come back in a week or so and do that. But alas, he had fallen ill of typhoid fever soon after and had never returned. Even now, though convalescing nicely, he was still confined to bed.

"If only poor Mother could know what Ernest had in mind!" Marie Melquiond whispered to Maria Candas shortly after midnight. "It would make things so much easier for her. But this way—"

"Maybe this way is the best way," said Maria gently. "The thought of dying in debt was always her greatest cross, you know. And if she carries it to the end. . . ."

Marie brushed away her tears. "Of course," she murmured. "I . . . I should have remembered that."

Then suddenly both women froze to attention. Pauline, a lovely smile upon her worn face, had begun to stretch out both arms towards Our Lady's statue.

"Mary, my Mother, I am all yours," she said, very distinctly.

The Daughters of Mary looked doubtfully at Father Rousselon who, for still another time, had completed the prayers for the dying. The end? But again the old priest shook his head. Undoubtedly Pauline had spoken her last words, but she was still clinging to life.

A few hours later, as the distant clocks of snow-clad Lyons began to chime the hour of four, he rose from his knees. "Now she's gone from us," he said quietly. "Look!"

"MARY, MY MOTHER, I AM ALL YOURS...."

The women drew near, and their eyes widened in astonishment. In the light of the single oil lamp burning in the sickroom Mother Pauline's face was radiant!

"Why, she ... she's *beautiful*!" exclaimed Sophie in awed tones. "And how young she looks! Not the least bit sick or tired. . . ."

Maria Dubouis smiled. "The saints are always beautiful," she said. "And young."

St. Meinrad, Indiana
Feast of Saint Dominic
August 4, 1952

HISTORICAL NOTE

Marie Pauline Jaricot was finally recognized as the foundress of the Society for the Propagation of the Faith on December 14, 1919, when the Society celebrated its one hundredth anniversary at Lyons. On June 18, 1930, her cause for beatification was introduced at Rome.

Ven. Pauline Jaricot
1799-1862

PRAYER FOR THE GLORIFICATION OF PAULINE JARICOT

O LORD, Thou dost will that all men be saved and come to the knowledge of the Truth. Thou didst inspire Pauline-Marie Jaricot to dedicate herself totally to the propagation of the Faith in the world. Do Thou hasten the day when Thy Church publicly recognizes the holiness of her life, that her example may draw many more Christians to spend themselves in proclaiming the Gospel, so that at last all peoples may know Thee, the one true God, and Him whom Thou hast sent, Jesus Christ Thy Son Our Lord. Amen.

IMPRIMATUR: ✠ Cardinal A. Renard
Archbishop of Lyon
Lyon, March 1, 1977

Those who receive favors or cures through the intercession of Venerable Pauline Jaricot are asked to inform:

Propagation of the Faith
12, rue Sala,
69287 Lyon, Cedex 02
France

By the same author . . .

6 GREAT CATHOLIC BOOKS FOR CHILDREN

. . . and for all young people ages 10 to 100!!

1137 THE CHILDREN OF FATIMA—And Our Lady's Message to the World. 162 pp. PB. 15 Illus. Impr. The wonderful story of Our Lady's appearances to little Jacinta, Francisco and Lucia at Fatima in 1917.   11.00

1138 THE CURÉ OF ARS—The Story of St. John Vianney, Patron Saint of Parish Priests. 211 pp. PB. 38 Illus. Impr. The many adventures that met young St. John Vianney when he set out to become a priest.   13.00

1139 THE LITTLE FLOWER—The Story of St. Therese of the Child Jesus. 167 pp. PB. 24 Illus. Impr. Tells what happened when little Therese decided to become a saint.   11.00

1140 PATRON SAINT OF FIRST COMMUNICANTS—The Story of Blessed Imelda Lambertini. 85 pp. PB. 14 Illus. Impr. Tells of the wonderful miracle God worked to answer little Imelda's prayer.   8.00

1141 THE MIRACULOUS MEDAL—The Story of Our Lady's Appearances to St. Catherine Labouré. 107 pp. PB. 21 Illus. Impr. The beautiful story of what happened when young Sister Catherine saw Our Lady.   9.00

1142 ST. LOUIS DE MONTFORT—The Story of Our Lady's Slave. 211 pp. PB. 20 Illus. Impr. The remarkable story of the priest who went around helping people become "slaves" of Jesus through Mary.   13.00

1136 ALL 6 BOOKS ABOVE (Reg. 65.00)   THE SET: 52.00

Prices subject to change.

U.S. & CAN. POST./HDLG.: $1-$10, add $3;
$10.01-$25, add $5; $25.01-$50, add $6; $50.01-$75, add $7;
$75.01-$150, add $8; $150.01 or more, add $10.

At your Bookdealer or direct from the Publisher.
Toll Free 1-800-437-5876   **Fax 815-226-7770**

6 <u>MORE</u> GREAT CATHOLIC BOOKS FOR CHILDREN

. . . and for all young people ages 10 to 100!!

1200 SAINT THOMAS AQUINAS—The Story of "The Dumb Ox." 81 pp. PB. 16 Illus. Impr. The remarkable story of how St. Thomas, called in school "The Dumb Ox," became the greatest Catholic teacher ever.   8.00

1201 SAINT CATHERINE OF SIENA—The Story of the Girl Who Saw Saints in the Sky. 65 pp. PB. 13 Illus. The amazing life of the most famous Catherine in the history of the Church.   7.00

1202 SAINT HYACINTH OF POLAND—The Story of The Apostle of the North. 189 pp. PB. 16 Illus. Impr. Shows how the holy Catholic Faith came to Poland, Lithuania, Prussia, Scandinavia and Russia.   13.00

1203 SAINT MARTIN DE PORRES—The Story of The Little Doctor of Lima, Peru. 122 pp. PB. 16 Illus. Impr. The incredible life and miracles of this black boy who became a great saint.   10.00

1204 SAINT ROSE OF LIMA—The Story of The First Canonized Saint of the Americas. 132 pp. PB. 13 Illus. Impr. The remarkable life of the little Rose of South America.   10.00

1205 PAULINE JARICOT—Foundress of the Living Rosary and The Society for the Propagation of the Faith. 244 pp. PB. 21 Illus. Impr. The story of a rich young girl and her many spiritual adventures.   15.00

1206 ALL 6 BOOKS ABOVE (Reg. 63.00)   THE SET: 50.00

Prices subject to change.

U.S. & CAN. POST./HDLG.: $1-$10, add $3;
$10.01-$25, add $5; $25.01-$50, add $6; $50.01-$75, add $7;
$75.01-$150, add $8; $150.01 or more, add $10.

At your Bookdealer or direct from the Publisher.
Toll Free 1-800-437-5876   ***Fax 815-226-7770***

MARY FABYAN WINDEATT

Mary Fabyan Windeatt could well be called the "storyteller of the saints," for such indeed she was. And she had a singular talent for bringing out doctrinal truths in her stories, so that without even realizing it, young readers would see the Catholic catechism come to life in the lives of the saints.

Mary Fabyan Windeatt wrote at least 21 books for children, plus the text of about 28 Catholic story coloring books. At one time there were over 175,000 copies of her books on the saints in circulation. She contributed a regular "Children's Page" to the monthly Dominican magazine, *The Torch*.

Miss Windeatt began her career of writing for the Catholic press around age 24. After graduating from San Diego State College in 1934, she had gone to New York looking for work in advertising. Not finding any, she sent a story to a Catholic magazine. It was accepted—and she continued to write. Eventually Miss Windeatt wrote for 33 magazines, contributing verse, articles, book reviews and short stories.

Having been born in 1910 in Regina, Saskatchewan, Canada, Mary Fabyan Windeatt received the Licentiate of Music degree from Mount Saint Vincent College in Halifax, Nova Scotia at age 17. With her family she moved to San Diego in that same year, 1927. In 1940 Miss Windeatt received an A.M. degree from Columbia University. Later, she lived with her mother near St. Meinrad's Abbey, St. Meinrad, Indiana. Mary Fabyan Windeatt died on November 20, 1979.

(Much of the above information is from Catholic Authors: Contemporary Biographical Sketches 1930-1947, *ed. by Matthew Hoehn, O.S.B., B.L.S., St. Mary's Abbey, Newark, N.J., 1957.)*